Transforming Through The

Human

Experience

The book information is catalogued as follows;
Author Name(s): Emma Louise Daniels
Title: Transforming Through the Human Experience
Description; First Edition

Book Design by Lynda Mangoro

ISBN (paperback) : 978-1-914447-43-3
ISBN (ebook) : 978-1-914447-44-0

Prepared by TGH International
www.TGHBooks.com

Transforming Through The

Human Experience

A guide to embodying your human experience,
to grow, learn and connect back to your authentic self

EMMA LOUISE DANIELS

The Voice

There is a voice inside you,

That whispers all day long,

I feel like this is right for me,

I know that this is wrong.

No teacher, preacher, parent, friend or wise man can decide...

What is right for you –

Just to listen to the voice that speaks inside.

(Author unknown)

Acknowledgements:

My heartfelt gratitude goes out to everyone who has supported me on my journey.

My wonderful parents, Mary and Alan, for their unwavering support and for always being there and for being the best grandparents Ava and Amelia could ask for.

My incredible sister, Joanne, who has and I'm sure always will be, by our side. She is an excellent guide for Ava and Amelia and an amazing support and non-judgemental sounding board for me! Thank you for being you, and for your contribution to this book.

My two daughters, Ava and Amelia. Without you, I wouldn't be the person I am today. I am proud to be your mum, and I can't wait to continue to travel along life's path with you. I love you both.

I would also like to say thank you to the other contributors of the book, Lyndsay and Deborah.

Deborah: The work you do and the love and dedication you do it with is truly remarkable. You and your wonderful team saved my life, and for that I am eternally grateful. Thank you for taking the time to contribute to this book.

Lyndsay: What a divine light! I can't begin to put into words what your guidance has given me. I was at my lowest ebb when I was guided to you and the beautiful work you do. I am forever grateful for your wisdom, your wit, and your beautiful soul. I am so proud to call you my friend.

Finally, I would like to thank Paul, my twin flame and incredible guide. We found each other in the most beautiful of ways; our journey together is just beginning.

Contents

Preface

*"If outside validation is your only source of nourishment,
you will be hungry for the rest of your life."*

I've always known that one day, I would share my story and write a book. However, I kept thinking: the timing needs to be right. The conditions need to be right. My headspace needs to be right. Suddenly, amidst the COVID-19 outbreak and the resulting social isolation and slowing down of life – the sentiment "there is no time like the present," couldn't have resonated more.

So here I am…

The journey of writing my truth to share with you has begun. It's Wednesday 18th March 2020. It's rather poignant for me that today is my sister's birthday. Joanne is one of the truly inspirational and uplifting women I have in my life. She has shared this journey with me through thick and thin. She has never wavered in her dedication and love for me and my two daughters and every day she continues to inspire, uplift and motivate me to be the best version of myself that I can be.

My intention for writing this book is from a place of gratitude. I am at a place in my life where I can authentically say that I am grateful for my experiences and the way that they have shaped me into the person who is writing this book today. I don't protest to be the finished product, who does? As human beings, we are constantly evolving, changing and learning through our experiences. However, I feel I am a much calmer and self-aware version of myself than I ever have been; this didn't happen over night and has taken dedication on my part to the ongoing process of self-awareness, inner child and shadow work.

Like everyone, I have had my fair share of ups and downs, and I have endured pain and suffering in various forms along the way. Comparison is the thief of joy. I do not seek to compare my journey with anyone else's, but simply to speak my truth and share my experiences in an attempt to comfort, raise awareness and empower you to step into your power, to not be ashamed of who you are, where you have come from, the experiences and mistakes that have shaped you, but most importantly for you to know that you are never alone.

Once you learn to trust that voice within, you will know you will always have yourself to fall back on. You are strong. You are capable. You have everything you need inside yourself to grow and become the best version of yourself that you can be.

In order to get to this place, you must want to get there. It is not an easy road and it is not a linear path. The process of deconditioning and healing from past experiences takes dedication, time and patience.

I am three years into my journey, and I am still travelling and finding bumps along the way. I am unsure of the exact moment that I lost my way and stopped trusting myself and my intuition, but leaving my ten-year marriage was the catalyst that made me realise I had indeed been on the wrong path.

I distinctly remember, once the shock had settled, sitting in the new house I had rented for me and my two daughters and thinking who I am really? It was a stark realisation that I had work to do, and this work was all inner work. As Singer says, in his incredible book The Untethered Soul, "your intuitive experience of what it's like to be you" is the only thing you should be interested in.

Everyone is on a unique journey and everyone's human experience is different. Put simply, you cannot fail at being you. It's just a matter of surrendering, and not allowing outside chatter to interfere.

I have spent a lot of my adult life trying to figure out what my purpose on this Earth is and what I need to learn from my experiences in order for aspects of my soul to grow and develop. What I have subsequently learned is, that this trying and pushing was indeed futile, and by responding and allowing life to come to me, I met much less resistance.

As Rumi said, "the inspiration you seek is already within you. Be silent and listen."

The path to enlightenment must start there.

For many of us, myself included, being silent and listening to our inner voice, or our intuition, or whatever we choose to call it, isn't something we have been used to doing. After all, this is not something we were taught as children; trusting ourselves isn't something that is encouraged as we grow; rather, as we grow, we become more and more conditioned to outside forces, energies and agendas and that voice inside of us becomes quieter and quieter - until we can no longer hear it.

However, from my experience, it is never too late to tune back in and listen. Spending time in your own energy is the most powerful way to do this; allowing yourself to work through painful emotions, traumatic events and remove blocked energy from your body in your own time, and in your own way, is one of the kindest things you can do for yourself.

My hope is that by sharing my experiences through this book, and some of the tools I have used to work through difficult experiences, you too will find the courage and the strength to live the life you deserve.

With lots of love,

Emma

Chapter One

"You're so afraid to hurt other people that you choose to hurt yourself by accepting everything"

- Ty Simmons

This sentiment was the way I lived my life for many years. In childhood I aimed to please my parents, and in adult life I was afraid to speak my truth and accepted everything - supressing my feelings in an attempt to keep the peace or keep everyone else happy.

Supressing any kind of emotion, either positive or negative, is never good. As Brene Brown tells us, "you can't selectively numb" emotions. I certainly learnt this the hard way. Since leaving my husband three years ago, I have been on an incredible journey of self-discovery, which continues every day. The road was rocky for a while and I came out of my marriage feeling vulnerable, lost and alone and during my time of self-realisation, I sat with a lot of very difficult emotions; it took me a very long time to work through them.

As I sit here now on Mothering Sunday 22Nd March 2020, in the midst of the COVID-19 outbreak and the onset of social distancing and home schooling, I am grateful that I am in the headspace I am in now and not the one I was in three years ago.

This is going to be a testing time for everyone.

On Wednesday evening, Boris Johnson, our Prime Minister, announced in his daily live press releases that all schools were to close for the foreseeable future in an attempt to curb the spread of COVID-19. As a single mother, with a ten-year-old daughter who has Williams Syndrome and an eight-year-old daughter, as well as being an English teacher in a pupil referral unit – this was a massive shock. They don't close schools. This must be bad. Then on Friday evening, Boris Johnson announced that all pubs, bars, restaurants and gyms were also to close for the foreseeable future too.

Social distancing is well underway.

This last week has been nothing short of surreal.

Surreal… I have now spiralled downward into anxiety and overthinking…

As a result of the above sentence, I took a 2 week break from writing. It's now Good Friday April 10th 2020. We have just come through to the other side of a super full moon, which was a highly charged and emotional one for me for many reasons.

Writing had to take a back seat.

The only time we should be leaving the house now is to shop for essential goods and for exercise once a day. However, for me and my girls, this means we must socially isolate for the next 12 weeks as my eldest daughter has been classified as high risk - if she were to get the virus due to her Williams Syndrome* (I will talk about this later) she could become very ill. Therefore, we must not leave the house at all or have any physical contact with any other human being for the next 12 weeks.

Our Prime Minister, Boris Johnson, has also contracted the virus and has only just been released from intensive care. However, he is said to be recovering well. These are scary and anxious times for everyone. Both myself and my girls, have struggled over the last few weeks with the negative energy and the fear narrative that is being spun by the media. As an empathetic person, this time is really testing me; so, we needed to fully retreat into ourselves and I needed to use all of our reserves and our toolkit of strategies to enable us to come through the other side.

I have been home schooling the girls and sticking to this routine, as much as we can, is highly important for us. We have been meditating, practicing yoga, being creative and exercising (thanks Joe Wicks for your virtual PE with Joe weekday morning workouts). In our home we now have a gratitude tree, a love butterfly and of course a rainbow in our living room window, which has become the symbol of hope through this pandemic.

Although I have had many offers of practical and emotional help from those closest to me, I am physically isolated from all other adult human beings. When the children are occupied or asleep, I am quite often alone with my own thoughts. I know I must stay strong for my children; the concept of digging deep and trusting myself to get us through this has never been more important.

As someone who has battled with her demons for over ten years, I felt I was coming to terms with who I was a person and starting to be kinder and more accepting of myself. However, like for many other people, this lockdown made old traumas resurface – a timely reminder perhaps, that I had not fully healed from them and that healing is in fact not a linear process, but more a rollercoaster of ups and downs that continues throughout your life. Being more self-aware allows you to sit with these emotions and work through them, but it doesn't mean that you are immune from setbacks when events such as the one we are living through right now happen.

Clearly, we are living through unprecedented times - times which are forcing each and every one of us to spend time alone with ourselves and our thoughts. There have been many a platitude on social media, claiming this time is a gift for us all; we must embrace the quieter and slower pace that life is now offering us, we must learn a new skill, we must grow in one way or another. However, whenever I read these platitudes I can't help going back to the same question: why can't we just be? Or at least do things at our own pace?

Now, more than ever, we need to be kind to ourselves. There is a time for being and a time for doing, which I have learnt much more about from reading Kirsty Gallagher's fascinating book Lunar Living. I would highly recommend this book to anyone, who wants to learn more about aligning their lives with the phases of the moon, and embracing the natural ebb and flow of life rather than resisting it.

For example, my default "hard on myself" inner dialogue was saying during those first few weeks of lockdown "why haven't you continued writing your book? What is wrong with you? Why are you so tired? You should be doing more!" Even though consciously I knew I shouldn't be beating myself up over this, I still was. I still hadn't fully learnt to be kind to myself and accept how I was feeling in that moment and that everything that was going on around me was affecting me.

What I should have been saying to myself was "You haven't continued writing your book because you have gone through an unprecedented amount of change. You are absorbing the negative energy that is everywhere and as an empathetic person this is making you exhausted. You are setting up a new home school routine for the children, as well as trying to be present for your work. You are trying to eat healthy, and stay active, you are trying to keep yourself and your two daughters physically and mentally healthy. Give yourself a break. There is no rush to write. When the time is right, the words will flow."

We hear the sentiment, "you should talk to yourself like you would your best friend, or your loved ones," often and although we get that on a conscious level, we don't always practice it in reality. However, I can tell you that when you are in lockdown, this is the biggest survival tool you have. You must talk kindly to yourself. Self-care in all its forms must take priority.

Sitting here in my back garden, on this glorious Good Friday whilst eating a delicious fruit salad that my daughter has spontaneously made for me, I realise that right now, despite what is going on outside of me, right now in this moment, my life is good. I know there will come a time when this lockdown is over and we will all resume our "normal" lives.

However, I think it is essential that we consider what "normal" is for us moving forward and what is so important that we must rush back to it. I am not a natural "let's just be" kind of person and I never have been, but this situation has forced me to adapt my mindset and realise that actually that's all there is right now.

I must just be.

Be present in the moment.

Be present for myself.

Be present for my children.

Right now, above all else, that's the only thing that really matters. I just hope that when all this over, we do take some of the lessons we have learnt through this lockdown into life moving forward – for me it will most certainly be to embrace a slower pace of life and to ride the waves of change and challenge without resistance.

Chapter Two

"The only certainty is uncertainty"

This morning, my meditation focused around the theme of uncertainty. This is the biggest challenge myself and many others are facing right now. When you have the desire to control events and outcomes in your life, uncertain situations cause you to become anxious. The COVID-19 pandemic is undoubtedly a cause for concern; however, it is the uncertainty that is causing many of us the most anguish.

This is what Tamara Levitt said during my meditation this morning:

"There are times in our life when we wake up to a world that is suddenly different. When we face this kind of turbulence in our lives, when everything is in flux, we scramble for certainty in whatever form we can find it. When we fear the unknown, we look for solid ground. But the truth is nothing is solid, everything is transitory and everything is constantly changing. Whether we are aware of it or not. This is important to remember, so while it is important to practice grounding activities like meditation, we also want to acknowledge the nature of change. Life is constantly changing, whether we want it to or not and no feeling is ever final. When we can learn to embrace uncertainty and remind ourselves over and over of the nature of impermanence, it can help us get through the most turbulent of times."

I needed to hear that today.

The concept of "scrambling for certainty" is something I can definitely resonate with, particularly since becoming a mother. Given my journey into motherhood (which I will share with you over the next few pages) and my daughter's diagnosis with a rare syndrome I had never even heard of before she was born, my brain has desperately tried to anchor back to a path of certainty and security. My journey into motherhood, and the journey I now share as a mother to my two daughters, is not the one I had carefully planned out in my mind. Honestly, having a daughter with complex needs wasn't something that was ever on my radar; my world was turned upside down when she was diagnosed at 14 months old. That wasn't even the biggest obstacle that my mind had to overcome. Prior to her being diagnosed, I suffered acute postpartum psychosis, again not something I had even heard of, let alone something I considered factoring into my birth plan!

So...

In terms of my journey into the unknown, I guess my first "real" encounter was after the birth of my first daughter, Ava, and my descent into an acute episode of postpartum psychosis. My pregnancy journey was very straight forward to the outside world. This was because I was physically healthy and my body coped incredibly well with the pregnancy. Like many women, I have had a turbulent relationship with my body though the years, but now, as I sit and reflect from a place of gratitude for all that she has endured and provided me with – I could not be prouder of her. Not once, during either of my pregnancies did my physical body let me down. Given all the inner work I have done on my mind, my body is reaping the benefits even more. I can safely say that at the tender age of 38, she has never been in better shape aesthetically, and more importantly she has never been more appreciated, loved and nurtured by me.

This wasn't an easy road, and it's one I will delve into later in this book.

For now, back to my first pregnancy. Outwardly, my pregnancy was going along swimmingly. The midwife was a little concerned that Ava was measuring small and so factored in a few extra scans along the way - "Nothing to worry about" I was told almost nonchalantly. However, inwardly I was worried. Very worried. So worried in fact, that I used to do secret internet searches looking for reasons why she may be smaller than average.

I never once spoke openly to anyone about this.

Why? You might ask. Even now, as I sit here writing this, I am asking my past self the very same question. Why? Why didn't you voice your concerns at this point? Why didn't you open up about what was going through your mind? Honestly, it was the fear of being judged. People telling me I was being ridiculous and there was nothing for me to be worrying about. Fear of people telling me to sit back, relax and enjoy the pregnancy. I have so much to be grateful for. And I did have so much to be grateful for, but I also knew deep down in my gut, that something wasn't quite right with my baby. I knew from when I was pregnant that she was going to be different. Could I have told you she was going to have

Williams Syndrome? No. Because I had never heard of Williams Syndrome. But, I knew she was different. They say a mother's intuition is never wrong. It's a shame sometimes that we don't trust it just that little more.

I can't tell you 100% that this inner anguish and turmoil inside my head was the onset of postpartum psychosis or indeed that this was a contributing factor to it – all I can tell you for certain, was that my intuition was speaking to me, and rather than listen to her and speaking my truth, I chose to supress and carry on as normal.

The birth of Ava was relatively uncomplicated (apart from the placenta not playing ball and deciding to stay put for a very long time!) Once that was all over, we were admitted to the ward.

Ava was the perfect little 5lbs 5oz baby, yet immediately, my worries resurfaced. How come she is so small when she is full term? Why can't I breast feed her? She also had to spend some time on the premature baby ward due to jaundice which, again, worried me a lot.

My exact memories of the days after Ava's birth are sketchy given the onset of psychosis beginning to take hold of my mind. Although, I don't have to try very hard to remember how I felt - the overriding feeling of growing paranoia. I became extremely paranoid that everyone was talking about me, looking at me and judging me. I remember constantly asking the midwives for reassurance and almost asking them to convince me that I was behaving "normally." I didn't feel particularly bonded with Ava at that point as I was so obsessed with feeding her and trying to get her to stop crying. To me, at that point, a new born baby crying was a symbol of my inherent failure as a new mother.

As the paranoia grew, that's when my hallucinations and intense claustrophobia kicked in. I cannot begin to describe to you the absolute terror I felt at the height of my episode. I was having horrendous panic attacks; I could hear voices inside my head telling me I must die, and I literally felt like I couldn't breathe. I kept forgetting Ava had been born and reliving the birth over and over again in my head, the agony felt real. Every. Single. Time. In the fleeting moments that I did remember she had been born, I didn't recognise her and the voices in my head where telling me I must die in order for her to live.

Postpartum Psychosis is defined on the NHS website as:

"A rare but serious mental illness that can affect a woman after she has had a baby. It is a serious mental illness that should be treated as an emergency."

Given my individual medical history, I was at about 0.1% risk of suffering with this mental illness - another reason why it was such a shock when it happened and nobody (and I am sad to say, not even the psychiatrist in the hospital who came to visit me) identified me as suffering with this. His diagnosis was simply "get a good night's sleep." Although this is sound advice, it wasn't the right advice at that particular time, and it certainly wasn't something I was able to do at that moment.

So... there I was trapped inside the hospital, trapped inside my mind, suffering acute postpartum psychosis and nobody seemed to know what to do.

As a result of a lack of diagnosis and, therefore, a lack of immediate treatment, my symptoms worsened. I began to feel Like Lady Macbeth, seeing blood everywhere in the hospital, all over the chairs and the beds and becoming increasingly paranoid and desperate to escape. Eventually, I did manage to leave the hospital and attempted to take my own life by throwing myself in front of the traffic outside the hospital.

It felt like my only escape.

Luckily, my husband at the time, pulled me out of the road and brought me to safety. It was at that point, that the hospital decided that they couldn't meet my needs and they decided to ship me off to a private clinic somewhere in Darlington. I think this was the point that I was sectioned under the mental health act.

I have vague memories of being transported in an ambulance from Dewsbury in West Yorkshire all the way to Darlington, with a midwife, a paramedic and my sister keeping me company on the way. I was in a very bad way at this point, and I know that this was a very difficult thing for my sister to endure. The only recollection I have of that journey was the ambulance driver pulling over so she could be sick.

This is the point at which I was separated from Ava, who was handed over to my parents to care for while I received treatment.

We were separated for around two weeks.

This is the worst thing that can happen.

Ideally, mothers who suffer with postpartum psychosis should be hospitalised in a specialist Mother and Baby Unit with their baby, but unfortunately due to various factors, this didn't happen for us. I spent one night in the private clinic in Newcastle and then I was sent back to a generic mental health ward in Leeds.

Again, this wasn't the right place for me and did not meet my needs. I have very vague recollections of holding a crumpled-up picture of Ava close to me during my stay there, a picture I had written her name on the back of, so I could remember who she was. I used to write myself notes too – lots of notes reminding myself that I had given birth to a little girl, and we had called her Ava Nicole. She was 5lb 5oz and was born at 4.26pm on Thursday 12th November 2009. It was so important for me to remember these things and I felt like my brain wasn't allowing me to. It was incredibly frustrating for me. I felt like I had to work so hard just to remember who my baby was.

By the time I had spent around two weeks on the ward in Leeds, I was ready to be discharged. Some very lovely doctors from the Mother and Baby Unit came to see me and this was the first time anyone told me that I had suffered postpartum psychosis. They said they now had a bed available for me at the unit and that they highly recommended that myself and Ava go and stay there, while I continued to recover.

Given that I had no idea what a Mother and Baby Unit was at that time, and the negative experiences I had endured so far, I just wanted to be discharged. Therefore, we made the decision for myself, Ava and my ex-husband to stay with my parents until I was well enough to transition back home.

If I knew then what I know now about Mother and Baby Units, I would have certainly taken up the offer of going to stay there. More on this later, as I recall the birth of my second daughter two years later. At that point, however, I was so scared and vulnerable that I didn't want to be in any more hospitals. I was convinced I would get well quickly if I just kept taking the medication and sleeping.

This is a major issue during psychosis and makes you realise just how important sleep is for your overall wellbeing. We know how important sleep is but still we don't really prioritise it as much as we could. We don't always factor it in to our health and wellbeing toolkit as something that is essential for us to function as human beings.

Literally, during that time, I would go three or four days without sleeping at all and even the sleep medication they gave me didn't work. The doctors kept saying over and over, if she doesn't sleep she won't get any better.

But, I just couldn't turn my mind off to sleep.

The mind. It's a bloody powerful tool isn't it?

I had never really thought about the power of the mind before I suffered with mental illness. I had never really thought about mental illness either if I am honest, as it wasn't something that I felt had ever impacted on me. Looking back now, with my personal experience, awareness, and the knowledge that I have gained over the past ten years, mental health and mental illness are always at the forefront of my mind. I am incredibly mindful of my own mental health and the mental health of my children and I strive to do my best to keep us all fit and healthy mentally as well as physically.

This has never been more important than right now, as we face this global pandemic together. All my tools have come to the forefront, especially when it has come to supporting my two daughters through the confusion of this, on top of trying to stay mentally well myself when I can't have any adult human contact - I have needed to dig deep and prioritise our self-care more than ever before.

For me, the biggest lesson I learnt through my first acute episode of mental illness, was how unpredictable it is. No matter how much you become aware of it and attempt preventive care and strategies, it can catch any of us out at any time, and it makes you incredibility vulnerable and reliant on other people for care and support. For someone as independent as me, that was a bitter pill to swallow. I had become so acutely unwell mentally, that not only could I not take care of myself, but I couldn't take care of my new born baby either. That was not only heart breaking, but also incredibly frightening. I had literally lost control of my mind and, therefore, my entire life and there was absolutely nothing I could do about it.

All I could do was surrender to it and hope that in time I would make a full recovery and regain my independence. This in itself was testing enough because on my road to recovery, I was constantly beating myself up, becoming highly frustrated and impatient with myself and feeling like a failure.

I remember coming out of the psychosis and looking at myself in the mirror for the first time in what felt like a lifetime. It was shocking. I didn't recognise the person staring back at me. My eyes were hollow and dark and I had never felt so exhausted in my whole entire life. It was like looking at a stranger. Coming out of postpartum psychosis for me, was like returning from an outer body experience and then being put back into the same body, but as a totally different person.

You are never the same again.

You recover and you're able to function and lead an independent life and all the rest of it, but that experience never leaves you. And I don't think it ever should. It shapes your future self in a way I am only now, ten years since my first experience, starting to fully realise. For many years, I didn't talk about it, I buried it and tried to pretend it didn't happen. I was ashamed. I felt guilty and I felt like people would blame me, saying I somehow deserved it, or brought it on myself for being a terrible person. That is genuinely how I felt.

Now, ten years on, I will openly talk about my experiences with mental illness, even if it's still a raw topic for me (and I think despite all the healing work I have done over the years, it always will be). However, I feel I need to be open about this major chapter in my life, if not for me, then for my daughters, who need to be aware of it for their futures too.

Chapter Three

"Williams Syndrome: A journey you never planned, but with the most amazing tour guide you could ever imagine"

In measurable terms, I had recovered extraordinarily well for my first episode of postpartum psychosis. I had managed to recover well within my 12-month maternity leave and was able to spend quality time with my daughter, doing "normal" maternity leave activities such as taking her to baby massage, toddler groups and the like.

However, I would be lying if I told you I thrived in these environments or really enjoyed them in the beginning; I didn't. I struggled through each social encounter and felt crippling anxiety every time I left the house with Ava. The reasons for this are multitudinous, but the main reason was because of my underlying feeling of constantly being judged and the fact that I didn't exactly feel "normal" whatever that means for a very long time. Due to my illness, my self-confidence and self-worth were at rock bottom. I felt "less than" all the time, and I was constantly comparing myself to other mums who seemingly had their shit together.

As I mentioned, Ava wasn't diagnosed with Williams Syndrome until she was 14 months old. We had a very difficult time with her as a baby, and that was aside from me recovering from psychosis; she struggled to feed and it would take up to 3 hours to get the tiniest bit of milk down her. I had given up breast feeding in the hospital - given the fact she couldn't latch on (another perceived failure of mine) and the fact that we ended up being separated from each other for around two weeks, meant it became a virtual impossibility anyway.

Ava WAS NOT an easy baby! Unknown to us at the time, she was actually intolerant to the formula milk I was feeding her as she was unable to digest it. This led to incredibly long feeding times, along with horrendous colic and constipation. I did take her to the doctor over this and mentioned it to my Health Advisor many times, but I genuinely felt like I was being "fobbed off" as a paranoid new mum (the irony!) and told she would be fine as it was very common in babies. Nevertheless, Ava would scream in agony all night, every night and no amount of colic massage was touching her. I felt awful for her. My Health Advisor diagnosed her as "failing to thrive." What an incredibly horrendous choice of language! If I didn't feel like a failure as a mum before, I certainly did after that.

So... despite being discharged and seemingly making an amazing recovery, I still had a niggling feeling that something wasn't quite right. At this time, I wasn't entirely sure if that was me or Ava, although my gut was telling me that it was Ava (like it had been all along!)

Ava had been diagnosed with hyperthyroidism at birth during the heel prick test and with a mild heart murmur at her six-week check at the GP. However, at this point, the doctors weren't joining up the dots and therefore Ava's Williams Syndrome was still some way off being diagnosed.

We struggled on, trying to downplay how incredibly difficult Ava was as a baby. We shouldn't be complaining so much right? New Motherhood is hard. Suck it up and crack on...right?

Therefore, I learnt to stop raising concerns about my daughter and kept quiet about my ongoing worries about her. I think many people, including those closest to me, thought I was actually paranoid as a result of my illness and therefore weren't really taking me seriously and dismissing my genuine concerns, because well she's bat shit crazy, isn't she? I am not going to lie, I used to find this incredibly frustrating, but my attempts to get people to listen to me at that point were futile so there really was nothing I could do.

In September 2010 when Ava was 10 months old, I returned to my job as an English teacher. Despite my worries about my daughter, I felt proud to be returning to the career that I loved after such an acute illness. I chose not to mention my psychosis to anyone at work. Looking back now, I think this decision stemmed from a place of fear and guilt. Fear that I would be judged and people wouldn't "get it" and guilt because - let's face it - becoming a new mum is the best time of your life and there must be something seriously wrong with you, if you become so acutely mentally unwell after having a baby.

It's important to bear in mind that my first experience with postpartum mental illness happened 10 years ago. I do believe that, at the time, there was a still a stigma attached to it which probably stemmed from a lack of awareness and understanding, particularly regarding the seriousness of postpartum psychosis.

Even now, when I read about the rare occasions where a new born baby has been left for dead outside a church, my first thought is never "what kind of a woman could do such a thing?" but rather, "where is this woman?" She is clearly acutely unwell and could be suffering from postpartum psychosis. I am of course not saying that this is the case all the time, however, in the cases where babies are left outside of churches for example, I do believe it could be.

One of my strongest memories from my first episode, was thinking I was hearing the voice of God, or in some cases the Devil. Links with religion, or feeling like you can hear religious voices, is a very common side effect of the illness. So, for a mother to leave her baby outside a church, in these circumstances, doesn't seem unusual to me as she will be thinking and feeling in her mind that this is the safest place to leave the baby.

As we have now moved on 10 years, I think society is becoming much more accepting of mental illness, and people are definitely more aware of it. Whether or not my feelings of guilt and fear would be lessened if, god forbid, I was ever to suffer again from postpartum psychosis is hard to say, but I do feel much more comfortable talking about my ongoing struggle with anxiety with less fear of judgement.

Everyone's story around anxiety is different, but I certainly believe mine is a lasting side-effect of suffering acute postpartum psychosis twice in two years. To enable people to understand this better, I always use the analogy of someone breaking their leg twice in the same place. Even if it fully heals on the outside, it will no doubt always be physically weaker and possibly prone to further injuries. I believe it's the same with the mind - you might make a seemingly full recovery from acute mental illness because you are able to function highly in society, but you may suffer with the side effects of psychosis, for example, which may manifest as anxiety and/or depression on and off for a lifetime.

Personally, my anxiety has never fully gone away, and I felt for a long time, that I must accept it as part of who I am, rather than trying to deny it, hide from it, or just hope that one day I won't ever have to face it again. However, as I have developed along my journey, I am starting to question whether or not it is a part of who I am or an element that I need to decondition from. Either way, anxiety has still played a major part on my story.

Due to the fact mental illness is invisible, I often think of my anxiety episodes as the lasting scar or wound on my brain opening up again. This reminds me that I always need to be aware of my mental health, I need to take care of it, accept it and work with it.

Looking back now, a lot of my ongoing struggles with anxiety have stemmed from not being true to my authentic self and not listening to my intuition. Suffering from acute postpartum psychosis (twice in two years) will do that to you.

It certainly rocks you to your very foundations and leaves you feeling weak, vulnerable, lost, ashamed and scared.

I felt like my sense of identity had been shattered.

I literally didn't know who I was anymore.

As I said earlier, as my psychosis started to subside, I didn't recognise the hollow-eyed woman staring back at me in the mirror. Obviously, my body had physically changed due to childbirth and medication; I had gained a substantial amount of weight. However, it wasn't about my physical appearance at that time. What I remember the most, was the empty, hollow greyness that seemed to be emitted from my body. My empathic traits mean I am very sensitive to energies - I can sense genuine feelings from just looking at photographs of people. Therefore, when I looked at myself in the mirror, on that particular day, the sadness and emptiness from inside was tangible to me. I felt like everyone around me could feel it and see it too. It was almost like the despair and blackness that was enveloping my body could be felt and caught by everyone who came into contact with me. Like the highly contagious COVID-19 virus, I felt like my broken soul could physically be felt and infect those around me. Therefore, I didn't want to be around people because I felt like I was a burden, my energy would drain them and I would leave them feeling as exhausted and debilitated as I felt. I felt like my entire being had been shattered and I didn't want those closest to me to feel the same pain that I was feeling.

Interestingly, since working on and cultivating my empathetic ability, this way of thinking makes total sense to me now. If you're an empath yourself, know anything about it, or anybody close to you has opened up about being one, you will know that this kind of experience is common for empaths. We literally absorb the energies of those around us, both positive and negative - this ability is another factor which can lead to a burnout, anxiety and depression.

As empaths, we can be great guides and serve others, but we must first be aware of this trait within ourselves, work with it, build our own boundaries and coping mechanisms, so as not to allow this amazing gift to be a detriment to us. It is only over the last year or so, that this has been brought to my attention as being part of who I am, so I still have some way to go in terms of educating myself and learning how to best make this work for me and those around me.

However, it has thrown light on the fact that ten years ago, it seemed entirely reasonable for me to assume that everyone would feel the same way as I did if they came into contact with me - at the time, I wasn't aware I was an empath and I wasn't aware that not everyone felt things as deeply as I did.

I knew from that moment on, my life was always going to be made up of at least two major parts: the Emma before my experiences with psychosis and the Emma after. It was going to take a hell of a lot of strength, courage and determination to pick myself up from this and rebuild my life.

Due to this inner turmoil, I wasn't strong enough to begin fighting for answers about Ava at that point. Even though I knew all along, right back from when I was pregnant, that Ava was going to be different, I silenced my intuition or allowed it to be silenced by external factors.

I have forgiven myself for this now, but it took a very long time to do so. It's also taken me a hell of a long time to trust my intuition again. I often ask myself if it's my trauma or my intuition which I am hearing, and it's taken so much work, a hell of a lot of work in fact, to start trusting my gut again. Aside from my sister, there is one another person I have to thank for that and her name is Lyndsay. She has been an incredible guide to me on my healing and spiritual journey. I have learnt so much from working with her. I am grateful she came into my life. You will hear more about her later in this book.

Given the fact I had seemingly fully recovered from my illness, I returned to work as planned in September 2010, when Ava was ten months old. Going back to work was a welcome release back to "normal" for me and provided me with a distraction. I will talk more about the pitfalls of distraction later in the book. However, at that point in my life, I have to say it was a very welcome distraction and allowed me to prove to everyone that all was "fine and dandy" and I was fully recovered. The "little check out" of my mind and sanity during my maternity leave was firmly rooted in the past, and it was something, those who knew about it with me, could forget about and move on from.

Except things are never really that simple, are they? More about that later.

Returning to teaching after maternity leave is never easy; returning to any job after maternity leave is never easy, but returning to work after suffering an acute episode of mental illness that your colleagues know nothing about, with a baby you are convinced has something "wrong" with her, is certainly not easy.

The "me" that retuned to work on that day in September 2010 certainly wasn't the same "me" that left ten months before to have my baby. I am forever grateful to have returned to a safe and supportive working environment, headed up by an amazing leader, who is still one of my lovely friends to this day. Without her support and care and the support of the fantastic team who I was lucky enough to spend a large part of my teaching career working alongside, my return to work would not have gone as smoothly as it did. That very common but very true saying "be kind, because you never know what secret battles people are facing" was never more profound to me than during that difficult transition back to work. Without the kindness of those colleagues around me, I probably wouldn't have survived and been able to flourish in a demanding teaching career for as long as I did.

I had been back at work for four months when we finally got Ava's diagnosis of Williams Syndrome in January 2011. We had been to a routine check-up with her endocrinologist just before her first birthday in November and he had asked the usual questions regarding meeting her milestones, such things as is she walking or crawling yet? The answer was no. This was now starting to raise some concerns for him, so he said he was going to take a blood sample from Ava to rule out "any underlying issues." He didn't elaborate further on this, and I didn't ask, so we had a further two months wait until the results came back.

The test for Williams Syndrome is a chromosome test - the blood is taken and inspected under a microscope. The genetic definition of the condition is that the person will have some chromosomes missing from chromosomes 7 (a tiny genetic deletion which is formed as soon as the sperm fertilises the egg) and occurs randomly in around 1 in 18,000 births in the UK. Williams Syndrome is non-hereditary and causes distinctive facial features and a range of learning difficulties. I believe it was these distinctive facial features that led Ava's endocrinologist to test for the condition.

So, we went away from the appointment having no clue that we would return in a couple of months and our world would be turned upside down.

I have always found questions regarding milestones interesting. I was regularly being asked about Ava's milestones, even in general conversation – anyone who is a parent will be able to relate to this. I said at the start of the book that comparison is the thief of joy. However, both during and after pregnancy, whether we like it or not, our babies are constantly being compared to each other, either from the professionals themselves, or by those parents we all know and love that we come across in baby and toddler groups.

I will always remember the red book; all parents will know what I am talking about here. The book you are given when your baby is born. It is the place where all of their medical records are kept and where the growth charts are - one of the tools the professionals use to diagnose your baby as "failing to thrive" if they fall below one of the growth lines on the generalised chart. Clearly, given Ava had WS, she never followed the growth curve in this red book, and I grew to hate it.

Many new parents will cherish it and keep it for a life, as a beautiful reminder of the early days. For me, it was a symbol of apparent failure as a mother as it served as a constant reminder that my baby girl was "failing to thrive" because she didn't follow the bloody growth curve in that stupid red book. The saddest part about this for me is that as soon as Ava was diagnosed with Williams Syndrome, she was given a blue book which was especially for babies with Williams Syndrome – what I would have done to have that book earlier on in her development rather than at 14 months old when she was finally diagnosed. It would have saved me a lot of internal angst and it certainly would have eradicated that horrendous phase from my story.

However, the lesson within all of that misery, was that I must learn to trust myself more and speak my truth regardless of what others may or may not think of me. This is always the lesson and this is something even now, I need to remind myself of from time to time.

Returning to the hospital in January 2011, for what we believed was a routine cardiology appointment for Ava, was the moment that everything changed. I remember vividly walking into the room and seeing the cardiologist sitting with two other professionals who I didn't recognise, but who I soon found out were a geneticist and a counsellor. What ensued is what can only be described as a whirlwind of information. We heard the diagnosis Williams Syndrome for the first time, and had no idea what it was, let alone what it meant for our 14-month daughter.

Despite the shock and surprise, the overwhelming feeling I remember taking away from that day was one of relief. It felt like although the journey we were about to embark on was scary and unknown, I finally had the answer I knew I'd been looking for ever since my pregnancy with Ava. The day we received the news was a blur to be honest and there was far too much information to digest about a syndrome we had never heard of.

The memory that stands out the most, was when one of the specialists handed over this enormous ring binder full of information about Williams Syndrome, including possible health and development complications for a person with WS from birth to death. It was way too overwhelming for me at that point and I remember throwing it in the bin when I returned home – perhaps an act of denial on my part at the time, but it's what I did and from that moment on, I decided that when it came to me and Ava, my intuition was always going to serve me better than anything else.

The ten years that myself and my family have been on this whirlwind journey with Williams Syndrome, has taught me a hell of a lot; not only about Williams Syndrome, but about myself too. There is no doubt that Ava is a unique, beautiful being, as we all are, but there is also no doubt that she faces many of her own personal challenges, which I have internalised as my own at times and often found it difficult to accept that we are two separate people with different destinies.

Whenever you become a parent, you are navigating an unknown field. You are getting to know a little human being (a being you brought into the world, yes) but also a being who comes into the world as an independent soul with their own destiny and truth. Our role as parents is simply to love, nurture, facilitate and guide them towards the life that was meant for them. Parenting is the hardest job in the world, and I have learnt that. As I write this, Ava is now ten and I continue to learn more about her, as I do with both of my daughters, every day.

However, I have learnt to embrace her quirkiness and I have learnt to let go of the fear that she might not "fit in" into this world; she may have challenges and struggles and she may be misunderstood and unhappy at times. This WILL happen for both my daughters, but this is part of their journey and their life. I am not here to micromanage the outcome of their life and wrap them in cotton wool, disability or no disability.

I am simply their mother, their guide and biggest cheerleader, not someone who can control outcomes for them in the future. It sounds really simple as I write it now, but my gosh has this taken some work for me to actually accept and let go of.

Most of this letting go has in fact nothing to do with the children at all but has to do with looking inward and exploring my relationship with myself and my perspective on the world. I have found my inner work revolutionary for my own personal awakening and self-healing journey. It is a step that cannot be ignored, not forever anyway!

Given my own struggles with mental illness and learning to come to terms with it, alongside learning to raise a little human with Williams Syndrome, has allowed me the space to learn, grow and develop my perspective on all aspects of life, including parenting. No two people have the same experience of life, even if they share some commonalities. Therefore, it is imperative that we understand and realise that our voice is unique in this world and we should use it and not allow it to be silenced either by our own inner critic or external factors. Everyone you meet knows something you don't and if you are open-minded, you can learn something from every single person you meet in life, especially your children.

Arguably, the world is saturated with opinions and beliefs about all aspects of life and, for a long time, due to feelings of low self-worth stemming from a number of other factors, I never felt confident enough to throw my hat in the ring and share my thoughts and opinions based on my unique experiences.

However, as a result of many years of dedication to inner work and trying to make sense of my past experiences, I was finally in a space where I could write my truth. My affirmations have always been:

I deserve to be happy.

I deserve to be respected.
I deserve to be heard.
I deserve to be seen.

The belief that this is true, however, took longer to sink in and become an inner truth, but with time, patience, practice and belief, it does happen.

Chapter Four

"Lightning never strikes twice…except it does!"

In February 2011, I fell pregnant again with my second daughter, Amelia Rose Papamichael, who was born in November that same year.

She is my little miracle.

Although we had tried for around six months to get pregnant with Ava, Amelia was an unexpected surprise. I am forever grateful for this, as I believe that if I had spent time overthinking a second pregnancy I may not have had her, due to my perinatal psychosis. I actually remember going to a scheduled meeting with a geneticist right after I had discovered I was pregnant again and she talked to me about my options if I did decide to have another child. When I told her I was already pregnant, she offered me an intrusive test which could determine if Amelia would have WS or not. However, there was a risk of miscarriage with this test. I declined it straight away, knowing that either way, I would be having my baby.

Unfortunately, the psychosis lightning bolt struck again.

I suffered again after the birth of my second daughter.

Although my pregnancy was very different, the illness hit around six days post-partum. However, my experience this time wasn't the same. I had been under the postpartum mental health team from early on in my pregnancy due to the risk it may happen again. I believe the risk statistically was greater for me, given that I had become pregnant again within two years.

The support I received from the team during my pregnancy was great, however looking back, I never fully engaged with the reality that the illness could (or would) strike again. As I didn't have any underlying anxiety around my second pregnancy, I felt much more relaxed and I had pretty much convinced myself that it wouldn't happen again.

The postpartum team had offered and prescribed me medication that I could take during the pregnancy to potentially prevent the onset of psychosis, but I refused to take it. Looking back there are many reasons for this, such as unknown side effects for the baby, risk of excessive weight gain, and my own personal struggles around taking prescribed medication. I remember, particularly the second time when I was in the midst of the psychosis, refusing point blank to take the medication prescribed to me – I was terrified of it – I felt like people were trying to poison me with it and it scared me to death. I think to the paranoid mind, this is quite common and something I am sure Mental Health Professionals deal with on a daily basis.

Therefore, my pregnancy with Amelia was a breeze and I very much enjoyed it. However, she was breech and didn't turn. So, on the 14th November 2011, I went back into the same hospital where I had given birth to Ava three years before to have my second baby via C-section. My only memory, of being in theatre, was one of the Doctor's asking me if I suffered with heart palpations and me replying with, "I don't think so why?" To which she said, your heart is racing and I said, "yes because I am shitting myself!"

Amelia was born at 1.15pm and weighed 6lb exactly. When she came out and was handed to me, the doctor pointed out straight away that she had a birthmark on the left side of her face. Immediately, I started to panic. Questions and thoughts started to flood my mind and I became anxious. However, in that moment, I managed to pull myself together and enjoy our precious first few moments together.

I spent two days on the ward in the hospital before I asked to be discharged. All the recommendations from my birth plan, such as having my own room etc. couldn't be facilitated due to the number of people in the hospital; I just wanted to be at home.

So, two days after the birth of my new born baby, I was sent home. Due to the birthmark on Amelia's face, we needed to return to the hospital for her to have a brain scan to double check that the birthmark wasn't causing her any brain damage. Thankfully it wasn't - the mark is just aesthetic.

My memory of that day is sketchy but there is one very vivid memory I have, which in hindsight was a stark warning that my psychosis was creeping in again. Given I had just endured major abdominal surgery, I was finding it painful to walk and so my parents had come with me to the hospital. I required a wheelchair to get around and I remember there was something wrong with the wheels on the chair and we were finding it difficult to manoeuvre.

Although this incident was mildly amusing, I found it absolutely and utterly hilarious. I remember laughing so hard, like The Joker from the Batman Films. The emotion was completely disproportionate to the incident and it was in no way balanced. This was the onset of my manic behaviour.

Unlike the psychosis I experienced with Ava, where my mind took me into the depths of hell and beyond, this time, my episode made me manic - I was on a perceived high for quite some time. My family recall my behaviour as somewhat amusing, if the circumstances of course weren't so tragic. I am unable to explain medically why this is; I am unsure that these things can ever fully be explained using just medical and scientific explanations alone.

I was told that perinatal psychosis is caused by an imbalance of hormones after the birth of a baby, and it usually occurs five days after the birth itself. The delayed onset of my psychosis after having Amelia was put down to her being born my C-section, which can delay the release of the hormones by a day or two apparently.

However, since working with my amazing spirit guide and coach, I have also come to consider alternative more spiritual interpretations of my illness, which I will explore later in the book. The medical explanations, although I am not disputing them, have never really satisfied by desire to fully understand the cause of such an illness, particularly for me personally. I feel since my spiritual awakening, I have been able to find much more self-awareness around the illness and it's allowed me to make peace with it, not only as part of my past, but also as part of my story.

Given that the onset of my psychosis was delayed, the acuteness of my episode didn't manifest until I was at home which was incredibly hard to manage for my family. I remember becoming increasingly more agitated and paranoid. The sad part for the sufferer is that it creeps up on you almost without warning and, although those around you can see that you are quickly becoming acutely unwell, you don't realise it yourself.

The community mental health crisis team came out to visit me at home. I distinctly remember this visit because I was utterly convinced that Lenny Henry and "that guy from The Office" Gareth Keenan (Mackenzie Crook) were sitting in my living room. I think I had convinced myself that I was famous and that for some reason I was being interviewed by them.

The psychiatrist from the Mother and Baby Unit then came out to assess me at home and diagnosed my psychosis saying I needed to be admitted to the MBU with Amelia as soon as possible. The only problem was that they didn't have space for me. Eight years ago, when I was suffering, there were six beds across the whole of Yorkshire and so bed space was at a premium. Luckily, they said they would have a bed available over the next few days and I needed to be "contained" at home until the time I could be admitted.

Again, I know this wasn't an easy task for my family. Despite having just had a C-Section, I was like a wild animal running around the house, not sleeping and apparently saying some very humourous things. Although I have no recollection of this, I used to write notes and leave them around the house. At one point, I had convinced myself that my then husband and father of my children was having an affair and so I had written a list of potential women I suspected. My sister tells me her name was on the list with the comment "no chance!" next to it - even if the midst of my psychosis, I hadn't completing lost my senses!

After a few days of fraught containment at home, the MBU were finally able to admit me. One of the many bizarre things about the psychosis for me, was that I was able to comprehensively direct my husband to the hospital, as I had been there a few times during routine check ups during my pregnancy. When I recall events such as this, it just reminds me how fascinating and amazing our minds actually are.

Despite suffering with two acute episodes of psychosis in my lifetime and consequently suffering the side effects of anxiety for the past ten years, it is only recently that I have actually started to properly research the mind, mental health but more particularly the subconscious mind. As Jung said: "Man is an enigma to himself" and this resonates with me. Although, I received outstanding care during my time in the MBU and I am under no illusions that the staff there saved my life, I was never fully satisfied with the medical explanations that were given to me around my illness.

When I arrived at the MBU, I was clearly at the height of my psychosis and had pretty much lost touch with reality. The wonderful and magical thing about the mother and baby units, is that they recognise the imperative need for you to remain with your baby, despite how ill you are. Once you arrive, you are given your own private room with a bed and cot and they aim to make it as nurturing and homely as possible for you.

I was acutely ill on my arrival so I required 24-hour surveillance. This was hard. My already paranoid mind was telling me that I was being watched constantly and being judged anyway, but when you arrive at the MBU this is actually the reality. You aren't given any privacy - a member of staff follows you literally wherever you go (and the ward isn't massive) and you must leave your bedroom door open. Although this is clearly for a good reason, I didn't see that at the time. All I felt was fear, paranoia and claustrophobia - all rolled into one. It was suffocating, it was terrifying and I had no idea why it was happening to me.

Again, sleeping was a huge issue; I just couldn't rest and my mind was on fire. Slowly, however, once the medication started to take effect and the psychosis subsided, I started to return back to reality.

The long hard road to recovery had begun again.

One day, I requested a visit into town to buy a Christmas dress for Amelia, as I was hoping to be discharged from the hospital before Christmas and I wanted her to have a pretty dress to wear. However, this trip into town when Amelia was around three weeks old, wasn't just about the dress. This was about me proving to myself to that I could do it. Proving to myself that I could walk, with my baby in the pram, into a packed town centre, go into a shop, choose a dress and come back again.

It sounds like such a simple act, doesn't it? An act that we all take for granted as something we do everyday (although as I write this we are in week ten of lockdown due to the 2020 global pandemic and, therefore, shops selling non-essential items still remain closed; a lot of things we have currently taken for granted are temporarily off the agenda for us.) However, trust me when I say, that as someone who suffered a second acute attack of perinatal psychosis, walking into Leeds City Centre that day with Amelia (with a nurse by my side) was one of the hardest things I have ever done in my life. The crowds. The noise. The overstimulation. It was exhausting. I almost turned back a few times but I was determined to prove to myself that I could do it. Guess what? I did do it, and I was bloody proud of myself.

I remember stepping into lift at one point and someone asking me how old my baby was, commenting, on "how amazing" I looked considering I had recently given birth. At the time, I was flattered by the comment and I took the compliment as it was intended and smiled. However, I remember thinking – I am dying inside. To the untrained eye looks can be deceptive.

Albeit, this wasn't the case with my psychiatrist at the MBU. I vividly remember one of my weekly meetings with him in particular. Each week, I met with him to talk about how I was feeling and to look at my medication etc. It was up to him and the team when I was allowed to be discharged from the hospital and I was desperate to get home for Christmas. So, even though I felt shockingly bad, I put a full face of make up on for this meeting, hoping to convince him that I was ready to be discharged. Needless to say, he wasn't fooled and actually told me straight!

However, given the amazing work that the MBU do, I did manage to return home for Christmas with Amelia that year so that we could all be together – however, I fully admit now that it was too early.

Although my psychotic symptoms had vanished, I had sunk into post-natal depression. Depression is something I had never experienced before, and it was horrendous. The MBU is able to care for women either in the hospital or in the community until their baby is 12 months old. I am unsure if there is a scientific or medical explanation for this, but I am guessing it has something to do with funding. As you can probably tell, I am not one for statistics. However, I am guessing that the "average" female recovers from perinatal depression within 12 months of giving birth, which is why specialist postpartum support for women is no longer available once your baby turns one years old. I was one of the lucky ones and thankfully my symptoms did subside before Amelia turned one, but this is not the case for all.

I know personally of a young woman, who had a baby son one month before I had Amelia, who unfortunately took her own life on discharge from the MBU. I distinctively remember her saying to me: "I will be the one who doesn't get better." It broke my heart to hear her say that, and I tried everything to reassure that she would get better but, unfortunately, she didn't. Her story is not mine to tell, however, it does show the severity of this illness and how heart breaking, debilitating and tragic it is. Although I did recover from my depression over the course of a few months, I distinctively remember how I felt - I can honestly say that if I had endured that pain for a very long time, I too could have taken my own life.

There may be some of you who can relate to the pain and anguish that depression brings, either through personal experience or through witnessing a loved one endure it. Even now, as I sit and write this book, it is hard for me to cast my mind and body back to how utterly horrendous I felt. Given the years of inner work and healing I have done, I do feel quite far removed now from that person I was then. I am acutely aware that I need to make self-care a priority in my life to ensure my emotional wellbeing is taken care of, and I realise that I am not suddenly immune to illness. Thankfully, as I write this, I haven't experienced an episode of depression like that again; as I have mentioned, I do battle with anxiety, but not depression.

However, casting my mind back to those dark days when I returned home with a one-month-old baby for Christmas, still breaks my heart. Amelia was able to spend her first Christmas at home with her two-year-old sister which is lovely, but if I am being honest, my memories of that time are vague. The transition back home with your baby is a crucial time, and one which requires patience, support and care. In fact, it actually starts with maybe one overnight stay in your home and then you return to the unit and it slowly builds up until the doctors feel like you are ready for discharge and into the care of the community mental health team. At first, I found this incredibly frustrating as I thought I was fine and was ready for the full transition back home, but I was wrong. It is such a precarious situation – it is not only your life that is potentially at risk, but that of your baby too.

So, I had returned home in December for Christmas, but I was still in touch with the Community Mental Health Nurse who was checking in with me weekly to ensure I was doing OK. She was an incredible support for me and would call round to see me if I felt like I was heading for crisis point. I was incredibly lucky to have a supportive network of people around me. Some women don't have that and, therefore, this link was vital.

My husband had returned to work in mid-January, and I was left on my own with both my daughters, for the first time since my illness. I struggled. Ava was two years old at the time, and on Tuesday mornings she would go to nursery as we had kept that routine going for her. I vividly remember one Tuesday morning, my husband had left to take Ava to nursery and it was just myself and Amelia in the house. As soon as he left, I felt terrified. I remember getting into the shower and having the most horrific panic attack. Immediately, I rang my husband and begged him to come back. It's such a hard feeling to articulate, but I was so fearful of being left on my own. I just couldn't do it. Whether it was because

I didn't trust myself with Amelia on my own, I can't really say, I just remember being a nervous wreck for quite some time and being unable to stay in the house alone.

Many people who have suffered with depression may tell you that mornings are the worst time of the day – I can vouch for that. I was struggling to sleep at the time anyway, but I remember thinking I don't want to go to sleep because I didn't want to endure that horrendous feeling again in the morning. Quite often, I would pray that I would die in my sleep. The days were incredibly long; I didn't have the motivation or energy to do anything and I literally couldn't see a purpose to my life. I am sure to many people this is incomprehensible for someone who has just had a baby and also has a two-year-old, but this is how I felt. This is how the illness made me feel. I remember I became obsessed with time. I was constantly looking at the clock, willing away the hours. Each minute was painful. I was dealing with the paradox of not wanting to be around people, but then struggling to be on my own. It was excruciating.

Things deteriorated to the point where I was readmitted to the mother and baby unit in February because I really was struggling to cope at home. Although other people may have seen this as a step back, I was actually incredibly relieved to be able to go back to the unit (I was lucky they had a bed for me) where I felt safe and secure, and I knew there was always going to be somebody around who could help me to take care of Amelia if I needed it.

Again, some of you might be thinking, "surely your home should be the place you feel the safest in the world?" I agree with you, especially now that I live alongside my two daughters in the lovely home I have created for us since my divorce, but back then, I hated the house I was living in, even when I was well, so those feelings were amplified during my illness.

The concept of home as an adult, has always been an interesting one for me. When myself and my husband bought our first house together, I felt like it wasn't really what I wanted. However, at the time, I was young and impressionable and I didn't really speak up about a lot of things. I had only recently graduated from university and my husband at the time was putting a fair amount of a deposit towards our home together by selling the house he already had. Therefore, in my conditioned mind, I felt like my opinion wasn't as important as his and I should be grateful for the fact we are buying a brand new four-bedroom, three-story town house. After all, isn't this one of the pillars of perceived success imposed on us by society?

In my heart and my gut, it never aligned with me, and I felt like I wasn't really able to put my mark on it. There was very little compromise when it came to decisions for the house and, in order to keep the peace, I never really spoke up for long. I persevered with it and it is where we had our two children, but I still never felt happy there.

When I made the decision to leave my husband, I left the house and pretty much everything in it; it held so many bad memories for me and was filled with negative energy. It was during that time that my attachment to material things started to really subside, and I realised that I was fine without them. I could rebuild my life from scratch with my children. In fact, when I left my husband I didn't have a job, or anywhere to live, but I distinctly remember the feeling of inner knowing that everything would work out in time. I will talk more about how this all worked out later in the book.

For now, back to my recovery. When I was readmitted in February, despite the feelings of safety and security I had within the unit, I was still getting frustrated with myself that my recovery didn't seem to be a linear process. I remember one of the nurses saying to me once, that I was being incredibly hard on myself and beating myself up along what was already a very difficult road to recovery. This is true and I have always been hard on myself and impatient with my progress. Even now, I need to remind myself to slow down and allow myself days where I can just be.

When you are in the grip of depression, allowing yourself to "just be" is excruciating because you feel so utterly hopeless and your mind is plagued by negative thought after negative thought. I remember one of the main reasons I was readmitted was so the professionals could do a review of my medication.

I am a solid believer and living example that medication alone is not the answer to mental illness, however, it certainly has its place and I was extremely lucky that mine could be monitored very closely in order to make it work for me. When I was readmitted to the unit, my anti-depressant medication was a relatively low dose, although I didn't realise this at the time. I remember when one of the nurses said to me that they had scope to increase my dosage quite considerably, I allowed hope to enter my mind again.

The downfall with any adjustment in medication of this type, is that once you start to take it, it unfortunately makes you feel worse before you feel better. This feeling can last up to two weeks and that amount of time, when you have depression, feels like a lifetime. In fact, you literally have to learn to take each moment at a time which is incredibly hard to do and takes so much focus and time. You pretty much know that you are going to feel utterly shocking first thing on a morning and that initial drag out of bed, is the hardest thing to do. You don't want to wash, you don't care what you look like, and you don't want to eat. Literally all the colour is drained out of your life. You actually feel numb. Neither happy nor sad. Just numb.

Sylvia Plath articulates it beautifully in her novel, The Bell Jar, when she says, "To the person in the bell jar, blank and stopped as a dead baby, the world itself is a bad dream." This is exactly how you feel inside when you are suffering with depression. You feel completely disconnected from the world around you, like you are sitting inside this bell jar observing the world without feeling or emotion. It doesn't matter what you currently have in life to be grateful for, such as two beautiful children, you can't feel gratitude – you are unable to feel anything. You are completely disconnected. Plath goes on to say, "because wherever I sat—on the deck of a ship or at a street café in Paris or Bangkok—I would be sitting under the same glass bell jar, stewing in my own sour air." Again, this articulates beautifully that this feeling is within you and cannot be changed by external factors. I could have been sitting on a Caribbean Island, with the sun beating down on my face and without a care in the world, but I would have still had that same metaphorical dark cloud hanging over my head. Until I recovered from this debilitating illness, I would be unable to enjoy anything in my life, including raising my children.

I can't remember exactly how long the depression had a hold on my mind, but it lasted a good few months and those few months were agony. My readmittance to the MBU lasted for one week only, but it was a big help in aiding my recovery. Once I was discharged, I didn't return. The medication was starting to take hold and this was obviously a positive thing. Slowly, I recovered to a point where I was able to function by myself and take care of myself and my children. I was by no means fully happy and aligned at this point though – far, far from it.

As I have said before, my belief is that medication can only bring you so far. Pregnancy had been a catalyst for my mental illness, a surge in hormones, but I do believe that my wounded inner child had also been crying out for help. There were so many issues that I needed to unpick and so much inner work that I needed to do, but at that time I just wasn't ready to face up to any of it. In fact, it would take me another eight years, to finally start making the changes that I needed in my life in order to find alignment with my authentic self.

I had been offered Cognitive Behaviour Therapy by the MBU, but by the time they had a space for me on the programme, I felt I didn't require it. Looking back, I do regret that decision and choosing to opt out of doing the inner work then. On the other hand, however, I may not have been ready at that time to make full use of the sessions and since meeting Lyndsay and working with her – I realise that the more holistic form of healing works best for me.

Despite suffering with psychosis and then post-natal depression, I pulled myself together enough to be at a point where I was able to return to work in September 2011. Again, I returned to the same job with mostly the same people, and again they had no idea what I had been through during my maternity leave. I returned to work on a part-time basis and, for a period of time, I was coping pretty well. The reason I say I was coping, rather than that I was happy and settled, is because that's exactly what it was during that time – putting one foot in front of the other just to provide for my family.

As I have said before, I had buried a lot of unresolved issues and looking back I was living my life in denial. There is only so long you can do this before you have to face up to it.

Chapter Five

"If neurotic is wanting two mutually exclusive things at one and the same time, then I'm neurotic as hell. I'll be flying back and forth between one mutually exclusive thing and another for the rest of my days."

- Sylvia Plath, The Bell Jar

For me, Plath succinctly sums up the plight of the modern woman in the above quote; highlighting the constant battles we face, from the external conditioning we receive to attempting to align and be true to our authentic selves. I, alongside many other women I am sure, had this constant inner battle going on between what external voices expected of me versus how I actually felt inside.

As a result of the inner work I have done over the years, I have come to the realisation that I am hugely susceptible to external conditioning around my sense of self. I used to think of this as a strength; I saw myself as a bit of a chameleon, someone who could fit into almost any social situation, someone who was inoffensive and would blend in quite easily with the people in my surroundings. I was pretty good at this and kept up the pretence for many years. However, when you don't really have a defined sense of self, there comes a point where you burn out. Every time you surrender to an external opinion or judgement that doesn't align with how you feel, a little piece of you dies inside. If you're not careful, you end up at 36 years old, having just plucked up the courage to leave your toxic ten-year marriage, looking in the mirror and saying: Who the hell am I and what makes me happy?

Conditioning starts from an early age and, unfortunately, there is no getting around it. As a parent, I am painfully aware of how my own conditioning can (and probably already has) conditioned my two children. However, through healing yourself and through conscious parenting, you can work alongside your children to alleviate the effects of this. Again, through my conscious healing work, I can raise my children, at the very least, with awareness and equip them with the tools they will need to eventually navigate this world alone.

During the period between returning to work after my second pregnancy and eventually taking the plunge and leaving my husband, I guess I was experiencing a slow realisation that internally I was very unhappy. Aside from what I had previously had to deal with, I was beginning to realise that my marriage was not a healthy one for many reasons. However, it took me a further six years to actually walk away from my marriage. Again, the reasons for this are multitudinous, but the emotions surrounding the prolonged decision to leave were fear, guilt, shame, anxiety and grief. I know first hand how hard it is to walk away from everything you've ever known and step into the unknown. I literally walked away from my marriage with nothing but the children, and needed to rebuild my life again.

However, before I got to that point, I was to endure another six years of attempting to fit into other people's boxes and making myself small, in a vain attempt to make my inevitably doomed marriage to work.

After the birth of Amelia and the medication I had been taking, I had put on quite a bit of weight and it was bothering me... a lot. I have sat with this a lot over the years and have really dug deep as to why it bothered me so much. Inevitably it comes back to having a weak sense of self and ultimately low self-worth. Societal conditioning again comes into play here, as we pin our worth on our external appearance. Before having the children, I never really had any body image issues. My mother always had a healthy relationship with her body and tried to instil a positive body image in us, so this wasn't something that was passed down from my family. It was something that developed in my head - a way that I could have some control over an aspect of my life when everything else felt out of my control.

It also didn't help that my then husband's family were obsessed with the external (in all aspects). I vividly remember the time his mum first met Ava. My ex-husband is half Greek Cypriot and his family, aside from his older brother, were living in Cyprus at the time. His mum had booked a flight to come over and meet Ava before she was even born, and she was bringing along two of his three sisters. At the time, this felt overwhelming for me as I had no idea what was going to happen to me after the birth, so I would have rather they waited to come over, but again I kept quiet - trying to keep the peace. So, I had just come out of the hospital and I was staying with my parents. I was feeling horrendous and I really wasn't up for visitors, nevertheless, I got Ava all dressed up in a little dress for her first meeting with her "Ya Ya."

I think I was wearing a tracksuit and I hadn't brushed my hair, but you know, I was recovering from an acute psychotic episode. Nevertheless - I digress.

On arrival, the first thing she said was, "Look at the state of you!" It's funny how so many of my memories have been lost, but this one has remained. Again, I think it's down to the feelings that you associate with a memory.

As the brilliant Maya Angelou said "People will forget what you said, people will forget what you did, but people will never forget how you made them feel." This is something that resonates deeply with me, and in the context of the above comment, is something that profoundly affected me. Of course, this sentiment works both ways, with positive feelings too, but when you are in a certain mindset, usually the self-sabotage mindset, you cling onto the negative comments and give them far more weight than you do the positive ones. It takes a hell of a lot work to shift the focus of your mindset from negative to positive, but with patience and practice you can do it.

That incident was one of a series of comments I had to endure from my ex-husband's family over the years. Therefore, when I had Amelia and realised I had gained weight, I wanted to lose it as fast as possible.

Over the past few years, I have worked hard to reconnect positively with my body and build a loving relationship with her. After all, she has never once let me down as the vessel that carries my soul in this human experience but, until quite recently, like many women, I would speak negatively about her.

During the time after Amelia's birth, I transferred my inherent unhappiness onto my physical body and blamed the fact that I had gained weight as the reason why I couldn't enjoy my life and be happy. It's that "when I am a size (whatever) again, I can be happy and enjoy days on the beach in my bikini with my children…" kind of internal dialogue that goes around and around in your head. The thing is though, that never works. I know from personal experience that if you don't fix the unhappiness inside, anything external will not fill that void; that includes your physical outward appearance.

At that time, however, I was slowly beginning to feel out of control; I was battling as a working mum with the pressures of a demanding job, raising my children, coming to terms with Ava's diagnosis of Williams Syndrome and also battling internally with the realisation that my husband probably wasn't right for me, and actually never was all along. There was a lot going on inside that head of mine and I wasn't ready to face any of it. Therefore, the weight loss journey became a distraction and it allowed me to regain some element of control. I, misguidedly, felt that by losing the weight and gaining compliments from society, that it would be the solution - that it would fix the constant pain that I carried around with me.

As a result, I did what many new mums have done and continue to do, I joined a slimming club. I signed up online and went along to one of the group meetings to collect the books etc. I felt so uncomfortable there it was unreal. It was all new to me, and it didn't sit right with me at all. Every ounce of my instinct was fighting against me being in this environment but, nevertheless, I persisted. I lined up to get "weighed in" and that's where my obsession with the number on the scales was born. For me, especially during that time, joining a slimming club was the worst thing I could have done for my mental health. I have quite an addictive personality and, at the time, I had a weak sense of self. When I put my mind to something I am quite relentless in my pursuit of seeing it through. The latter of course is not always a bad thing, but given this context of me falling into the clutches of diet culture when I was very vulnerable, it wasn't great.

However, I am grateful that four years on from my experience, the anti-diet movement is creating huge waves and making progress for our younger generations. We still have a long way to go in terms of education and awareness, but I am a strong believer that starts at home.

As a mother of two, I feel it's essential that as my children grow up, they see a mother who is comfortable with her body, who honours her body, and who has a positive healthy relationship with her body.

Four years ago, I was not that mother. Four years ago, the girls would have seen a mother obsessively weighing herself up to 15 times a day; they would have seen a mother who was starving herself aspiring to an unobtainable image of herself that she had allowed to be created by external voices; they would have seen a mother who suffocated her natural love of food in an attempt to feel worthy. They would have seen a miserable mother.

At this point in my life, I hadn't discovered my love and passion for training and yoga and therefore I was attempting to control my weight purely through what I was eating. The thing is – it worked! I successfully lost around three to four stone and shrunk from a size 14/16 to around a size 8/10 in UK clothes size. If I am really honest, when I look back at pictures of myself from that time, for a glimmer of a moment, I think you look good there Emma, but then I remember how I felt and I remember for a woman of my height and stature that body shape isn't sustainable for me – the sacrifices I had to make to maintain it are just not worth it.

I remember the crescendo of events that led up to my sister sitting down with me and telling me how worried she was about me. My sister knows how much I enjoy food and she could see how I had begun regularly declining foods that I would normally enjoy because I was trying to lose weight. She could also see how much weight I had already lost and that I couldn't actually see if myself. That's the thing – you become addicted to the weight loss and the only thing that matters is the number on the scale.

There is one particular memory that stands out to me, of when we were in Cyprus visiting my ex-husbands family. One of the only perks to these traumatic trips was the Greek food. I adore Greek food and there was never a shortage of it on our trips over there. In fact, everything was to the excess. I remember a particular poignant comment that my ex-mother in law made during one meal time, when there were quite a few potatoes left, "give them to Emma" she said "she will eat the whole bowl." During that particular trip, I was on my strict diet and so I was doing my best to "be good" as they say. I remember eating a few salad leaves and rushing into the bathroom to weigh myself straight after. If I wasn't satisfied with the number on the scales, I would start doing sit ups or push ups on the bathroom floor and then weigh myself again. Literally, the number on those scales would make or break my day, my mood, my entire perception of myself. It was exhausting, debilitating and impossible to maintain.

I had developed a very unhealthy relationship with my body and with food and something needed to change. After my sister's firm words, and the fact that I hadn't really fully taken them onboard, my ex-husband actually threw our home weighing scales in the bin. This was the best thing he could have done for me to be honest, and it was this action that was needed for me to slowly begin to develop a healthy relationship with my body and food again.

My unhealthy relationship with my body and my addiction to diet culture is not something I have struggled with my whole life. Therefore, rightly or wrongly, I believe it is a side effect of my mental illness after having my babies. There is no doubt my body had changed. I had been taking powerful medication that can induce weight gain, I wasn't eating particularly well when I was ill, and I had given birth. However, by no means was I obese and my weight wasn't putting my physical health at risk – it was my mind that was allowing the negative noise from outside to infiltrate my sense of self-worth because I had gained a few pounds. Again, because I wasn't in the headspace where I was being kind and compassionate to myself, I was beating myself up and therefore I was desperate to change my physical appearance quickly. The problem was that I didn't do this in a healthy way and I was placing far too much emphasis on it, to the point where it was impacting negatively on all aspects on my life.

Luckily for me, I had a sister who was willing to tell me the truth and make me reflect on my behaviour as unhealthy. Although it took time, I did do this and slowly my addiction to weight loss subsided and, once I found training, I found that I was able to maintain a healthy weight without the need to starve myself.

I am not saying that, despite the inner work I have done over the years, that this demon doesn't sometimes rear its ugly head. Through my work with Lyndsay, I have consciously accepted that I am very susceptible to outside conditioning. We are all susceptible to outside conditioning to varying degrees; it is something none of us can escape from. However, when you lack a stable sense of self, which I did for many years, this conditioning from outside is even more powerful and can infiltrate you when you least expect it.

Here is an example. For about three years now, and until the pandemic hit (which closed all the gyms) I had been an avid member of the gym and aimed to train three to four times a week. Towards the back end of last year, I had hit a bit of a plateau in my training and needed some motivation. Around that time a new Personal Trainer had joined the gym. I had attended one of his classes and thought he would be a good person to rejuvenate my training programme and give me the push I needed to get my momentum going again. So, I hired him as my personal trainer.

He's a very experienced trainer and highly experienced body builder. I told him my goals and he set me a training and nutrition programme. The plan was very restrictive and in my heart of hearts, I knew it wasn't going to be good for my mental health. Again, because it worked in changing my body shape, it would have been very easy for me to slip back into my old patterns because my body was physically changing. I was getting complimented on my physical appearance, however, inside I was miserable.

It really hit me, when I realised I wasn't able to share a meal with my children; they were starting to notice and asking me why I was eating "different" food to them. The young impressionable teenagers I was working with at the pupil referral unit were also noticing it. Given the pupil referral unit is a nurture school, we would sit around the dining table and eat breakfast and lunch together, and when they started to notice I wasn't eating bread anymore they were asking me why - I couldn't really give them a convincing answer because I was actually thinking, "God knows why I am not eating bread…I love bread!" Sitting around the breakfast table, while they were tucking into boiled eggs on toast, was torture for me… and actually it wasn't worth it! I wanted to be a positive role model for the students and to be able to enjoy food again, so I thought this has to stop.

The reason I tell this story is two-fold really. The first reason, is because this episode was as recent as the beginning of this year (2020) and you'd think that at 38 and given my history, I wouldn't put myself in that position again, but it's so easy to slip back into these toxic patterns if you allow the conditioning and outside noise to penetrate. Luckily, this didn't go on for too long, and the gyms closing due to the pandemic actually came at the right time for me, as it allowed me space to pause and say this isn't what I want - this isn't making me happy and I have two daughters, who are looking to me to have a loving and positive relationship with my body and not be somebody who is punishing my body, making myself miserable and aspiring to the unobtainable. Therefore, with forgiveness, I was able to close that chapter on my life with relatively little harm done.

The second reason is that, bearing in mind, I can be an all or nothing kind of person, I had to admit to myself that I had substituted my addiction to controlling the food I eat to an addiction to training.

Consciously at the time, I wasn't aware of this and even if I was, I was justifying it away by saying to myself there are worse things to be addicted to which I came to realise after my divorce. I spiralled into toxic habits, such as binge drinking, in an attempt to validate my existence, distract from my reality and avoid actually sitting with the discomfort of my feelings and working through them. More on this later.

I think one of the reasons I was able to spot this potential downward spiral was that I had taken the time to do some inner work and I was already well on my way with the healing journey. I had explored issues around my body and, looking back through my journals around that time, I had written a lot about this. I would like to share a few things I wrote with you. The first one was my personal definition of "the perfect body." This is what I wrote:

It starts with our relationship with our body and how we talk about our body, both internally and externally. After all, the body is simply a shell that carries around our human consciousnesses and is the vessel that allows us to have a human experience. However, she is a beautiful and sacred vessel, unique to us and amazing in her capabilities. Therefore, I must learn to nurture her, nourish her, respect her and love her, that way whatever shape or form she takes over the years, I will honour and respect her, and she will continue to serve me how she is meant to.

The other thing I did, which was a recommendation from the self-help book: The Inner Fix, was to write a letter to my body explaining to her all the ways I had neglected her over the years, explaining how I will do better, ask her forgiveness, forgive myself for the past and make promises about how I will aim to do better.

This is my letter:

Dear Body,

These are some of the ways I have neglected you in the past:

Smoking.

Drinking.

Starving you.

Talking negatively about you.

Not allowing you enough rest and sleep.

Training too hard.

Neglecting your skin.

Eating badly.

Letting men exploit you.

I would like to ask your forgiveness for the ways I have neglected you and talked negatively about you. I have abused you, and for that I am truly sorry.

From now on, I will cherish and love you for the great and incredibly beauty that you are. You allowed me to birth two beautiful babies, and you have allowed me to remain physically active throughout my life. You have NEVER ONCE let me down. You are a warrior and I am proud of you.

From now on I promise:

I will slow down and get more sleep.

I will nourish you with healthy food and drink and I will listen intuitively to what you need.

I will never allow an unworthy man access to you EVER AGAIN.

I will drink plenty of water.

I will continue yoga, which you clearly enjoy!

I will show you off and be proud of you.

I will not speak negatively about you.

Most importantly, I will love you, enjoy you and continue to watch you flourish.

I love you.

Emma

This might not seem like anything major, but it's actually incredibly powerful and healing. It's a personal and private contract between you and your body, which allows you to build up that positive loving relationship with your body that you may have lost. It's also a way of keeping you on track when you might feel like you're slipping into old patterns; you could almost think of your body as your accountability partner, someone who is on your side, your best friend and someone who just wants you to love and accept them for who and what they are.

I found it an incredibility healing experience.

Given that I had already started the ground work in reclaiming self- love for my body, lockdown allowed me the time and space to reflect on my previous relationship to exercise, and consider whether or not it was a truly healthy connection. Clearly, I was using the gym excessively as a coping mechanism, to distract me from my difficult emotions, but lockdown meant that rug was pulled from underneath all of us. Therefore, I was given the gift of time to develop a more loving and healthy connection to the movement of my body.

I discovered yoga about a year before lockdown because my body was screaming out for it, and that, combined with meditation, was a lifesaver during the pandemic. Many of us know the benefits of yoga but, for a long time, I thought I was someone who couldn't get on board with it – it was too slow for me! I needed HIIT training and to push my body to its limits. I am by no means saying the two are mutually exclusive - you can be a lover of yoga and meditation and smash the hell out of a bootcamp (which I still do) but I wanted to get to the root cause of why I was resisting yoga and why I was unable to slow down and allow myself time to build it into my daily routine.

The reason was fairly simple - I didn't want to sit with my emotions because it was too uncomfortable.

Yoga is incredibly healing if you allow it to be, and during those early weeks and months, after I left my husband, I couldn't sit with myself long enough to do it. However, my body and soul must have known intuitively that I would need the benefits of yoga very soon, and so I pushed myself to keep trying. I started with videos on YouTube and found the fabulousness of Yoga with Adriene and just by practicing 20 mins a day using her videos, my practice improved immensely and I can honestly say I couldn't be without it now. Especially during those intense three months of lockdown, which I will talk about in more depth later in the book, yoga kept me grounded. It gave my thinking mind a break and allowed me to fully come into my body and reconnect. Amongst all the confusion the pandemic brought to the world and to individuals alike, yoga was a great place to land; I will be forever grateful that I found its benefits before lockdown and was able to nurture and grow my relationship with it, as well as encouraging the girls to use it as tool too.

Chapter Six

"Not everything that's faced can be changed, but nothing can be changed that is not faced."

- James Baldwin

The internal struggles I have had with my addictive relationship to food and exercise stemmed from a lack of contentment and inner peace, and a desire to keep control of something when I felt like my life was spiralling out of control. After I had my daughters and I returned to work as a teacher in 2012, I became like many other working mums – extremely busy and extremely stressed.

My life at that point was definitely in survival mode and I didn't feel particularly supported or connected to my husband. I am not going to slate my ex-husband or blame him entirely for the breakdown of our marriage, but what I will say is that during the years leading up to me making the decision to leave, we were not on the same page about many things.

Parenthood changes you. There's no doubt about that. You have to step up and accept that your life is totally different now you have children. Every marriage, every parent and every family are on their own path and you can't compare situations, all you can do is talk from your own personal experience. Our situation was more complicated than most, given my episodes of postpartum psychosis and our daughter being diagnosed with a rare syndrome. A lot happened for both of us. In the space of three years, we had gone from a newly married couple, to a couple who now had two children and the remnants of psychosis to deal with.

When I reflect on my ten-year marriage, I have to be honest and say, we were never really compatible from the start. I don't blame my ex-husband for this, as I have to hold my hands up and say that even before we married there were red flags popping up that I chose to ignore. For example, the first time we went to Cyprus to meet his family, which was around 3 months after we met, it wasn't exactly enjoyable for me. I put this down to the drinking culture of the family. The biggest lesson I learnt through all of this is that if it feels wrong, it probably is wrong. They weren't necessarily bad people, they just weren't my type of people. However, because I was 23 and a people pleaser with a precarious sense of self, I allowed myself to be swept along with it and convinced myself that it was all good.

I realise that I am reflecting on these times with the power and advantage of hindsight, but even at the time, I didn't feel as happy as I probably should have. I justified away a lot of my ex-husband's actions, like when he turned up visibly hungover to our wedding day and how his family arrived late to the ceremony and completely took over the entire event and he never once stood up for me, or what I wanted. The bottom line is I didn't feel seen. I didn't feel heard and I didn't feel respected. This was always going to be a recipe for disaster.

Despite the traumatic start to motherhood that I had, I did recover fairly well from my psychotic episode after the birth of Ava, and all I really longed for was a sense of peace and a calm environment to raise my baby. As I have said already, for most, parenthood fundamentally changes us, as we need to adapt to the needs of our new born. For my ex, however, life pretty much remained the same. He would be out in the nightclubs until the early hours of the morning, and he would invite his friends around for games nights that went on until 5am in the morning. This just didn't gel with me - it wasn't the life I wanted and deep down I knew it. However, I wasn't ready to confront it, or accept it was happening.

I vividly remember a time when Ava was just six months old, we went away on a holiday to Cyprus with two other couples and their children. We didn't have Ava's diagnosis of Williams Syndrome at the time, which unbeknownst to me will have been playing subconsciously on my mind. We stayed in a complex in Ayia Napa; it was a very beautiful resort but, even then, I constantly had this sense of unease around me – maybe due to the fact I still didn't have answers about Ava and I was still, when you put it into perspective, in the early stages of my recovery from psychosis. It was also because I wasn't hugely familiar with one of the couples we were going with and, although they were very lovely people, my insecurities and worries around external judgement, and the fact that Ava was a challenging baby, were playing heavily on my mind. Although we were going abroad under the pretence of this being a family holiday, I knew deep down it wouldn't be like that at all.

One example of this from the holiday is when we were all sitting in a very noisy bar on evening, while the football was on. Ava was screaming, and when I mean screaming I mean that you could hear her easily over the music, the football game and the chatter in the bar. I know now the reason that she was struggling so much in the noisy bar was due to her hyperacusis, which is a symptom of Williams Syndrome and is to do with how you perceive sound. Sufferers experience a heightened sensitivity to particular sounds that are not usually a problem for other people. Repeatedly, I was saying to my ex-husband we need to leave the bar as Ava is really struggling. The response I got? "Well you're her mum, you should be able to calm her down!" Wow! What ensued was his clear refusal to leave the bar, and myself and Ava walking all the way through Ayia Napa alone back to the apartment. In isolation, that incident might not seem like much, but that was the flavour of many incidents in my life.

Most of our family holidays were spent in Cyprus visiting the Greek family. For anyone who has family abroad, especially a large family, you will understand when I say that visiting them, no matter how beautiful the country is, doesn't constitute a holiday – well not my idea of a holiday anyway. It's hard work.

Even with the girls in tow, we would be up until 5am in the morning "partying" in family houses, which wasn't a healthy environment for anyone. Mainly because these family gatherings always descended into chaos, often with two of the sisters getting so blind drunk they would be arguing and shouting at each other for no real conceivable reason. It's amazing when I look back at what these so-called holidays were like for me. There were many times when me and the girls would be left in the apartment alone, so my ex-husband could go out partying with his sisters and brother until the early hours of the morning. He would then refuse to get up when the girls wanted to go and play in the pool or go to the beach. Alcohol was literally the centre of the universe for his family. Granted, they were brought up in a bar in the tourist area of Cyprus and so it was very much part of their culture, but it almost felt like they couldn't make it through a gathering without being drunk.

Now, don't get me wrong, I am not averse to the odd drink and I do enjoy socialising to an extent, but to me this felt out of control and the reasons they were drinking so much, in my opinion, weren't the right ones. However, rather than project my issues and judge the family, I needed to look inward at what the excessive amount of alcohol was triggering in me and felt like it was MY relationship with alcohol that was something that I had to sit with. It played such a pivotal role in my ex-husband's life that there was no way I could ignore it anymore. I have to say, that there were times when I adopted the "if you can't beat them join them" mentality and there have been many occasions in my life where I have been very drunk. In fact, I do believe that if I hadn't left my marriage when I did, I was very much in danger of becoming an alcoholic.

In fact, the word alcohol is said to have come from the Arabic term, "Al-Kuhl" and "Al-Gawl" which means "body eating spirit." Whether this is true or not, I know from my own personal experience that this definition resonates with me. Drinking alcohol is one of the fastest, easiest and indeed culturally acceptable ways you can lower your vibration and keep your human consciousness in a lowered state. For me, it made decision-making even harder, heightened my anxiety, lowered my patience , made me feel groggy for days afterwards and gave me so much brain fog that I didn't have the energy to even accept that I had created this reality for myself, let alone the energy to find clarity and take the action I needed to make the situation better.

This is where people get stuck – they give away their personal power to others, don't take personal responsibility for the direction of their life, blame others and fail to act. I am not going to lie and say accepting fully that you have created your reality is easy. It's not. It takes courage, strength, resilience, forgiveness and a firm belief in yourself that you can do it. When you are constantly under the influence of alcohol, it makes this journey even harder, to the point where rather than accept that something needs to change and then make the change, people just settle for the mediocre - thinking there is no other way.

There is no denying that alcohol plays a big part in our society and our social lives. This has never been more prevalent that in the current pandemic. As I write this, all bars, pubs and clubs have been forced to close their doors for three months and many people are going crazy. I know that when I was with my husband, my entire social life revolved around it, even when we were not on holiday.

Towards the end of our marriage, my husband had converted our integral garage into a fully stocked bar, complete with disco light, smoke machine, the lot. Although it looked very impressive and drew the crowds, it wasn't really something I wanted in my home. I wanted to use that space for a sensory/play room for our daughters, but that wasn't meant to be.

Once the bar was installed, that gave my husband licence to invite people around every Friday night to get blathered in the bar until the early hours – bearing in mind this place was also doubling up as my family home. There were many Friday evenings where I just wanted to put the girls to bed, have a bath and a single glass of wine, put on my PJ's and chill in front of the TV, but if I dared as much as to suggest this I was branded boring. So, I caved and we would have guests in the house almost every single Friday night, and I would ultimately end up drinking more than I wanted to and feeling hungover and unproductive for the next day – I hated it.

I seemed to be getting myself into a bit of a cycle, almost using the alcohol to numb out the pain and emptiness I was feeling inside. A dangerous downward spiral. I know I must take responsibility for that, and I have done. Nobody was forcing the drink down my throat but, ultimately, I was feeling trapped, lost and alone.

Intrinsically, I do believe that I am an introvert who has been masquerading as an extrovert for almost her entire life – no wonder I felt drained and lost when I left my marriage. Since my post-natal illness, I also suffered a lot with social anxiety, which for anyone who suffers with it knows how crippling and debilitating this can be. Therefore, alcohol was a way of supressing those feelings and it allowed me to display apparent confidence and self-assurance and let go of my inhibitions. Catherine Grey articulates this beautifully in her book "The Unexpected Joy of Being Sober" where she talks about her battle with alcoholism.

I found that even in my own home, when guests were coming into my space, my social anxiety would rear its ugly head. This was probably due to the fact that the people who were entering my home didn't feel like safe people to me; what I mean by that is that they didn't really get me and, therefore, even in my own home which is supposedly the safest space in the world and the place where you can truly be your authentic self, I felt very much out of place.

Unsurprisingly, the final push I needed to finally call time on my marriage had at the very heart of it, alcohol. There had been a slow build up over the years of incidents that I was uncomfortable with and I felt that, after ten years of trying to make it work, I was tired. Leaving my husband wasn't something that I woke up one morning and impulsively decided to do. I fully appreciated and understood that this was a huge decision and one which was made even more complicated by the fact I had two young children, one of whom has special needs. However, in my mind I had tried everything.

Around three years or so before I took the decision to leave, my anxiety was creeping in and I was struggling to cope with work, the children and my manic home life, which revolved around drinking with little time for proper rest. During that time, my mental health deteriorated to the point where I was signed off work. Whilst at home, I attempted to speak to my husband about our situation and how I was feeling. His response was that I was failing to cope with being a mother and a teacher and he basically gave me an ultimatum, claiming it was either the job or my family. This hit me hard at a time when I was incredibly vulnerable and trying everything I could to feel back in control again. After careful thought, I decided to hand my notice in at work and take six months off work.

At the time, those closest to me were saying what a fabulous opportunity this was, I should enjoy the quality time with the children and the time I will have for myself when they are at school. I have to admit that my passion for fitness was something that was born out of this time and is something I will be forever grateful for, but it didn't change the fact that in my mind I had just given up on a career I adored because my husband had told me I couldn't cope, and I believed him.

During that time of my life, much of my identity and feeling of self-worth was wrapped up in the fact I was a teacher. I realise now that my worth isn't determined by external labels such as wife, mother, teacher and so on, but rather comes from within. Yet at the time, and due to the fact that it hadn't really been my decision to leave the profession, I felt like a failure.

I felt so much like a failure in fact, that I was even struggling to do the school run. For four years, I was a parent governor at the girls' primary school - a role I very much enjoyed. However, even as a governor, I can see that the school playground can be an intimating place, not only for the children but for the adults as well. There is a clear social playground hierarchy that is hard to ignore and it is a gutter for gossip and low vibrations. Therefore, for someone with social anxiety, it is a nightmare to navigate.

When I first started taking the girls to school, after I took sick leave from work, people would be asking questions such as "oh, are you not at work today then?" "I thought your parents did the school run?" "Is everything OK?" Although these are seemingly well-intentioned questions, they used to send my inner dialogue into overdrive and my anxiety out of control to the point where I was utterly exhausted when I returned home.

After a few weeks of feeling this way, I decided I needed to act in order to try and ease the burden for myself, so I decided to join my local gym. Up until this point, I had never really been into fitness - even at school I wasn't a fan of Physical Education and would do anything I could to get out of it. One thing I had always enjoyed though was swimming and it was something I had done as a child. So, my plan was to join the gym so that when I dropped the girls off at school, I would head straight there to do a few lengths of the pool, then come home. The hope was that this would help improve my anxiety. I cannot begin to tell you how hard the first few times were for me; I was forcing myself through the motions of dropping the girls, driving to the gym, swimming 50 lengths, and returning home. At the beginning it was almost robotic. I didn't interact with anyone at all. I literally was in and out. Despite this, I always felt that little bit better on my return home.

Consistency was key for me during those early days, along with patience. I wasn't enjoying it at first - I was enduring it in the hope that eventually I would start to enjoy it. And guess what? After a couple of weeks of consistently going swimming every morning after the school run, I did start to feel better and slowly started to enjoy it. I also started interacting more with the people around me and decided that I would try some of the fitness classes. Although I had no idea what I was letting myself in for when I first entered a Les Mills Body Pump Class, I have never looked back!

Up until that point, I had never done any form of resistance training at all and I rocked up to that class like a lamb to the slaughter. The most vivid memory I have of that first class I took part in, was the female instructor leading the class and how bloody awesome I thought she was. She inspired me, encouraged me to keep going. I thought she looks like a woman who has her shit together - I wanted to be like her!

If I was to pinpoint a moment where I realised the power of fitness on mental health, that would be it. It was in that moment that my passion for fitness was born. I think the reason that I have been able to stick to it, is that my motivation has NEVER been aesthetic. My original motivation for joining the gym was to improve my mental health, and that continues to be the reason I train. Of course, my body changed as a result of the training but, for me, it was almost an unnoticed side effect at the beginning because my focus was always how I felt after a training session, not what I looked like or a number on the scales.

I am grateful to have found a gym that knew how to make newcomers like me feel comfortable. It's intimidating enough walking into a fitness class for the first time, surrounded by people you don't know, who in your "self-sabotage mindset" look better than you, but when you are already crippled with anxiety, looking around and comparing yourself negatively to the other women in the class - it's even harder.

Gyms have got the power to be transformative places for both physical and mental health, but they also have the capacity to be dangerous places too if the vibe isn't right. It's one thing going into the gym so that you can be the best version of yourself outside of the gym, but it's quite another if you go to the gym, in the hopes of transforming yourself into an unattainable image that you have seen a social influencer post on Instagram. We all have our own personal responsibility to be healthily connected to the gym and understand what it can do for our health and wellbeing, but I also feel gyms have a collective responsibility to provide a safe and nurturing environment for people to develop healthy relationships with their body, their minds and their relationship with food and nutrition.

The power of exercise on mental health is never more prevalent than as I write this. We are now three months into lockdown and, therefore, the gyms have been closed for three months. Unfortunately, this has had a tremendous effect on the mental health of people who rely on the gym as a tool to keep their mental health in check. Personally, I have made a conscious effort to practice yoga every day at home, and the Joe Wicks workouts have helped me immensely. However, I don't believe there is a substitute for a good workout with a group of like-minded people and an instructor who knows how to push you. In fact, as I write this, my body is still recovering from my first group outdoor bootcamp session that was organised by my personal trainer that I attended yesterday. It felt amazing to be training again with people from the gym and being pushed in a way I hadn't been for three months – there really is no substitute for it in my mind. Although it was painful, it was just what I needed and I felt re-energised, optimistic and grateful for a return to some kind of normality. It has definitely reminded me of the power of training for me. It was clear from the mood, energy and vibe of the class, that everyone was feeling the same and was looking forward to the gyms reopening (hopefully in the next few weeks!)

As I have already written, before my final decision to leave my marriage, I tried to make changes that I thought might help save it and one of those was eventually handing in my notice during my sick leave. Despite the school doing everything they could to keep me at that time, I felt I had to leave to try and save my marriage, as my husband had convinced me that it was my inability to cope with a demanding teaching job and family life that meant that we were struggling. Therefore, I left with no idea what I was going to do next. To be fair, my mental health was fragile and so taking some time out of work to focus on myself and my girls was something I needed to do.

Once I found the gym and got into a new routine, I was feeling fairly settled and after around six months, I was itching to get back to work again. During my time as a member of the gym, I had signed myself up to complete a Level 2 Gym Instructor Qualification, as I wanted to keep my brain active and I love to learn. I also noticed that the gym was advertising for a sales consultant and so I decided to apply. I managed to secure the job and started working there in November 2017. Although I was grateful to have the job and I enjoyed the interaction with the staff and the clients, I quickly realised it wasn't for me. My vocation is, and always has been, working with young people in some capacity or another and my family life hadn't really improved even though I had scarified my career to try and change it. I was working long shifts at the gym which often included weekend work – something I wasn't used to doing. Therefore, the work didn't really suit family life. Additionally, my husband wasn't really pulling his weight and was continuing to drink and socialise in the house bar, even on Saturday evenings when he knew I had to be up for work on a Sunday.

It still wasn't working.

Therefore, on Mother's Day in March 2018 everything came to a head. Typically, we had my husband's family over for the Saturday evening, which included his brother and his relatively new partner, his sister and her relatively new partner, and his other sister who was visiting from Cyprus. The plan was they were going to come over for the evening and then his brother's partner would drive them all back to their house, as she wasn't drinking. That was not what happened. The family, as usual, ended up getting blind drunk and kept on drinking until the very early hours of the morning. As usual, I had put the children to bed, and left them to it downstairs, going to bed myself. By the time my husband came up to bed, I was fast asleep and so we hadn't had time to chat. I assumed that all the guests had left, as per the arrangement, so when Ava came in to get me to take her for her breakfast, I took her downstairs. When I opened the living room door, I couldn't believe what I was seeing. His sister and her partner were sprawled out on the sofa, he was completely naked, and the house was a tip. Immediately, I pulled the door shut and went back upstairs. I woke my husband up and told him what myself and our eight-year-old daughter had just witnessed downstairs, but his response was "chill out, you're overreacting." At that moment, something just snapped inside me, and I realised I couldn't do this anymore.

Calmly, I gathered the children together and we went to my parents' house. There, I broke down and explained exactly what had happened and how I had been feeling. They listened without judgement, at that point and told me whatever I decided to do they would support me.

I decided I needed time and I needed space.

Therefore, I returned home and explained this to my husband the clearest way I knew how and I asked him if he would respect my wishes and leave the house for a bit, so that I could think. At first, he refused point blank to leave, but eventually he said he would go stay with his friend for a bit. However, the entire time, he was bombarding me with messages such as "I need to know what our relationship status is, as I have dates lined up," and turning up unannounced at the house. I remember one occasion, where he had clearly been out drinking, he let himself back into the house late in the evening and got into bed with me. I just couldn't cope.

After a very short space of time, he declared that there wasn't anything more to think about and he was moving back into the house. It was at that point, that I took the children and went to stay with my parents. Since that moment, I have never been back into that house.

So, there I was. No home and no job – I had handed my notice in at the gym at the beginning of March because I realised it wasn't working out for me. Despite the apparent rock bottom I had hit, I had an inner knowing that everything was going to be OK, and it was.

I knew I wanted to get back into teaching.

It has now been three years since I left my husband and, although we are still not officially divorced at the time I write this due to issues sorting out finances, my life is much more in alignment. My daughters are happy and settled and I am managing to hold down a full-time teaching job, as well as raising the children. It just goes to show the absolute catastrophic effect a toxic partner can have on your life and your potential. The biggest lesson I have learnt from period, is that if we are unhappy or unfulfilled, we must look at our life, be responsible for it and then begin to change it.

It's taken me three years and a global pandemic to finally feel like I am somewhat healed from my past experiences, but the lessons I take with me moving forward are invaluable. I move into the next phase of my life with gratitude, forgiveness and a renewed sense of purpose.

Chapter Seven

"Growth is painful, change is painful, but nothing is as painful as staying the same."

- Dr Sebi

At the time when I walked out of my family home and away my husband, my children with me, I didn't even have a job because I had recently handed my notice in at the gym. Unlike my decision to leave my marriage, which I internally agonised over for a very long time, my decision to leave the gym was fairly impulsive. I knew in my heart it wasn't where I was supposed to be; I was missing my vocation of teaching and longed to get back to it in some capacity or another.

Despite this time of incredible uncertainty, I had an overwhelming sense that this was what I needed to do and, although it would be painful beyond belief, my ship was finally pointing in the right direction.

We were safe in the sense we had a roof over our heads at my parents, so I could focus on finding myself a job. I remember meeting with my wonderful mentor and friend, Caroline, who pointed me in the direction of the school where I work now. We met for lunch and she told me about the teacher of English role at a pupil referral unit, suggesting it would be a perfect match for me. I made enquires, went to look around, applied for the role and was successful. I had managed to secure a permanent position with a good salary to begin the following September.

In order to see me through until then, I signed up to a supply agency and I was able to secure long-term supply work from April-July, which allowed me to save some money to rent a property in the summer. As I write this, we have been living in this house for two years and, although this is a rental property, I feel so at home here. This is the first time I have fully been able to be in my own energy and create a space that feels like me. The girls have settled in well and also feel at home here.

Given that we are just coming to the end of a five-month lockdown, I could not be more grateful for this safe and sacred place that we now call our home. Although I don't own this property, it feels more like home than my other house ever did. We are all so conditioned by society that we must "settle down", get a massive mortgage tied around our necks and work to pay it off for the rest of our lives in a bid for "security."

However, if we really unpick this, we must ask ourselves where does this sense of security really come from? It doesn't come from the external world, it comes from within. Personally, I feel much more "secure" and settled living in this smaller rental home on my own with my children than I have done in my entire life. This is our space. Me and my girls have created the energy and it feels beautiful.

It has now been just over three years since I left my marriage and the family home. We are still not officially divorced because my ex-husband is very focused on material possessions and perceived "winning", therefore we are currently locked in a legal battle. If this time has taught me anything at all, it is that the universe always has your back. Trust in its power, align yourself with your true self; don't get too attached to the external world, and you won't go far wrong. Although the legalities of my divorce are still not final, I have made peace with that and I have forgiven my ex-husband for the way he is continuing to behave towards the finances of our marriage. What will be will be; if we both end up with nothing in terms of material possessions from the marriage, then so be it. I have my children, and we have our health and our freedom. The anchors of the past only weigh us down and I have worked through my feelings of anger, bitterness and resentment, to finally be able to say that right now, in this present moment, everything is OK.

I trust myself and I trust my path.

Now, don't get me wrong, I didn't just arrive at this sense of inner peace the moment I left. It has taken a LOT of hard work, a lot of mistakes and a lot of soul searching to get me to this point. I am still learning and growing all the time, which I will continue to do until the day I die.

The biggest realisation I remember having when I left my marriage, was that I didn't know who I was anymore. I didn't know what I liked and what I didn't like, I didn't trust myself – I felt utterly lost and lonely. I use the word "lonely" specifically, as opposed to "alone", because at that time lonely was exactly how I felt. I struggled to be in my own company, as I had never lived alone in my entire life, and there I was at 36 moving into a house by myself with my two children.

During those early days, I would constantly keep myself "busy" to help distract myself from my current reality and what was going on inside my body. I found it impossible to sit in stillness with my emotions - it was too painful. I would hit the gym as many times a week as I could and I would distract myself with my work, but the most debilitating distraction I used, which is a common one, was alcohol. The children would go and spend every alternative weekend at their dad's and this was the trigger for me to go out drinking.

The worst part about this time in my life, was that I wasn't enjoying the drinking and the partying at all. I suffered with "social anxiety" which was shocking, especially the day after. I have memories of myself getting ready for these nights out thinking I really don't want to go. So why did I? Because I was lost, sad and searching from some kind of external validation or connection with something or someone outside of myself.

It was during this time, that I hit some real personal low points.

I was drinking myself into oblivion and I would feel dreadful afterwards. It's taken me a long time to forgive myself for this dark post-marriage period of my life. Deep down, I knew this wasn't me, it was not fulfilling and it couldn't continue. I had to take charge and start taking responsibility for my life, my past decisions and my future direction.

But first, I needed to get myself sorted inside.

This is where my great spiritual coach, and I would like to say friend, Lyndsay came in. My wonderful sister introduced to me to her when she could see I was struggling and she has been such an integral and inspiring part of my journey.

As you can imagine, throughout my adult life, I have had many encounters with therapists and psychiatrists, but I have never met anybody quite as unique as Lyndsay. Lyndsay is the founder of Sacred Moon Wellbeing Centre, which is located in a little village called Horbury in West Yorkshire. As soon as I met her, I felt an instant connection with her and knew she would be able to guide me.

I would describe Lyndsay as my spiritual coach, guiding me back to my own intuition.

One of my earliest memories of visiting her was when I experienced one of her own unique therapies which is called EAT (Ego-Avoidance Therapy.) When I first went to see Lyndsay, I had an overwhelming feeling of guilt surrounding the fact that I was the one that had ended the marriage and ultimately given my children their first "traumatic experience" of being products of a "broken home."

I put these descriptions in speech marks very deliberately because, at the time, I was very much plugged into the matrix and so I was struggling with this dilemma internally. Now, however, I feel that these terms are very much a part of societies conditioning on us. I have worked hard to heal the conditioning since leaving my husband and through my work with Lyndsay, have slowly been able to bring myself back to the metaphorical home of my inner truth.

This next section is the beautiful soul that is Lyndsay explaining what Ego Avoidance Therapy actually is:

"I feel really honoured that I can explain something about me and what I do. I birthed Ego Avoidance Therapy through studying CBT. Due to the fact I am always connected to a source and my guides, I remember doing some sessions with my clients and being able to see the energy in their bodies - it was almost like my guides would take me to where this energy was dense and looked dark within their body. When I was sitting talking to my clients, I would think there is something that is stuck, something in the emotional body, or pain body, that has to be acknowledged. As a result of this, I began experimenting a bit with my own intuition and my guides and tapping into that frequency and my auric fields. This wasn't something that I would see with my visual eyes - it was more an inner knowing; I really had to trust that.

Therefore, when Emma used to have the sessions, it would be a case of getting her into almost a meditative state to come out of her mind and go into the actual feeling - I think that's something that people find really hard to do. I think the reason people find this so hard is because we are so conditioned to live through what our mind tells us as an authority, when really, it is our emotional body that is constantly our frequency and transmitted to guide us about where we are at.

For example, when Emma came for her sessions, I felt that her frequency was her conditioning from other people, her partner, her mum and dad and the people around her. What I genuinely felt was that this was so far removed from what her truth is; she had almost suppressed what she wanted to say back to people as her truth and that was sat as a heavy energy in her body.

Emma would come for a session with say a feeling of guilt, but that guilt wasn't actually her guilt, or it could have been guilt that she wished she had spoken her truth or said no, but she didn't recognise that at the time.

I feel it's important for me to highlight that this technique very much comes from spirit. One of the most important things to take away from this, however, is that if you suppress your truth it will sit stagnant in your body and that could then lead to physical ailments, for example back ache. Your body is desperate for you to connect with it, and I feel that is how true self-love is birthed. For example, my recent back ache was actually a feeling that I needed to attend to and once I practiced the EAT technique on myself, by going into my body and into the feeling and attending to it, the back ache disappeared. The mind is hugely responsible for ailments that drop down into the emotional body, or pain body. I would describe EAT as a tool to access your emotions and your inner truth, to self-actualise and as a form of self-inquiry. It is a way to bypass the ego, and access the emotions and the feelings that the ego is telling you not to."

I remember vividly my first ever EAT session with Lyndsay. I had arrived feeling "heavy" and my body was tight and aching. As we sat and talked, I was able to pinpoint the feeling in my body which, for me, is nearly always the stomach. Lyndsay asked me what colour and texture it was and how it felt in my body. Through Lyndsay's guidance, I was able to turn the feeling into a different colour and allow it to dissipate in my body. The energetic shift I felt after this process was literally immediate. Instantly, my body felt lighter and the pain in my stomach had disappeared. It was an incredible feeling. EAT therapy allowed me to apply all the theoretical concepts I have read about in such books as "The Power of Now" by Eckart Tolle about being "in the body" and allowing the inner body to guide you to higher consciousness. However, sometimes, when you are reading such books as the aforementioned, you can become confused and swamped by the concepts being described. My advice would be to actually try some of the practices out for yourself. Personally, I needed the guidance of someone as experienced and "awake" as Lyndsay to be able to guide me in this when I first started. Personally, although everyone is on their own unique journey with this, I believe the more we can connect with likeminded "awake" individuals the more powerful the practice becomes, as it reminds us about the "collective consciousness" and how we are all ultimately connected. By raising our own vibration, we can raise the vibration of these around us and of the universe as a whole. As Eckart Tolle says, "It is easy to stay present as the observer of your mind when you are deeply rooted within your body." So, if you are interested in raising your vibrations and are constantly on the quest for inner peace, start by rooting yourself within your body daily.

Everything you require for inner peace is within you. Your body is crying out for connection.

Finding Lyndsay, and the Sacred Moon Wellbeing Centre, has allowed me to practice and learn the techniques of being more present by reconnecting with my body and dissociating or transcending the mind. My time in lockdown has also allowed me the time and space to apply daily practices, such as yoga and meditation, to really allow myself the opportunity to reside in the role of the observer and just "be" rather than "do."

It truly is a transformational process and I am forever grateful for the space the universe has given me to accelerate my healing process.

I do not profess to be an expert in psychology, or in the workings of the mind. However, I have a lot of personal experience in this area and, since my experience of psychosis, I find it fascinating. Therefore, I have done extensive research of my own around the concept of the ego, conditioning and spiritual ideas. Put simply, the ego is the "I." It is how you see yourself. Your ego is the unconscious part of your mind and identifies with beliefs, traits and habits. Your ego develops as a false construct of how you identify yourself - this develops through childhood and becomes stronger through outside conditioning.

None of us are exempt from external conditioning, and even the most conscious parent will condition their children – it's part of life.

However, when you start to explore the concept of the ego, you realise that doing this work should not be "the death of the ego". Instead, for us to become the conscious observer of our ego so that we can consciously detach from that part of ourselves, which with practice, brings about a state of inner peace. There are many fabulous people who are highly qualified in offering coaching around Ego Work. If you find yourself in any way "stuck" or repeating negative patterns, whether that is professionally or in relationships, looking more deeply into Ego Work may benefit you. Your ego identifies "I" through external things such as your physical body, the job you have, the car you drive, the house you live in, how many children you have. Even your name.

I have experienced this quite profoundly a couple of times in my life. The first time was when I had my children; it seemed that it was it for me, that was now all I was. My entire identity was "mother." This concept never sat well with me, yet since doing the healing work, I resonate with this concept even less.

Another example, was when I left my teaching job, as previously explained. The reason I think I struggled with this so much was because I was having what the brilliant Erica, The Queen of Confidence, calls an "identity fuck." That part of my ego that identified as a teacher was panicking like mad, because if I wasn't a teacher, was my "I" now worth less? What would others think of me? Had I now failed at life? As the conscious observer of my thoughts, I can see my ego was well and truly running the show at that point in my life. Now, I can sit back and observe thoughts such as these, as they arise, knowing that the true essence of who I am is the conscious observer of my thoughts and no matter what my external identity is, at any point in my life, it does not determine my worth. Life is transient and external situations change. The biggest lesson for me, is to never to attach your self-worth to external things, because if, for whatever reason, something changes, which it inevitably will, you will be less equipped to deal with it - your ego will take over and you will no doubt end up suffering as a result.

Since being on my healing journey, I have reflected on my past quite extensively. Not to dwell on it, but rather to learn from it with conscious awareness. One thing I have realised, when I look back at my life and particularly the big decisions I have made, is that many of them have not come from my truth or what I wanted out of MY human experience. In fact, most of them, for example getting a job straight after university when I wanted to take a year out to travel first, then buying a big house with a huge mortgage, then getting married in a church, were all decisions that were very much taken out of my hands and imposed on me from society, or by my parents.

When I reflect on my past, I often think about The Butterfly Effect. One decision could change the entire course of your life path and the path of others. At the age of 21, if I had been "allowed" by my parents to take a year off to travel with my boyfriend from university like I wanted to, the course of my life could have been very different indeed.

Due to my personal circumstances, I have reflected on the course of my life and I have been forced to question all kinds of things, including my upbringing and conditioning of my parents. You can't hide from your past forever and in order to be in the present moment and be content in the present moment, I think it's imperative that you sit with and unpick your programming and thought patterns, so that you can become conscious of these and reparent yourself in a way that allows you to be the best version of yourself moving forward.

Also, as a parent myself, I have found it invaluable to become awakened to my own conditioning, so that I can consciously parent my girls. As I have already said, none of us will ever be free of external conditioning, it is a part of life, but I believe the more we educate ourselves as parents around our own conditioning, the more we can be open and honest with our children as they grow and develop and align with their own individual paths.

My journey back to myself with two little girls by my side has not been as easy one and it has been slow and painful in many ways. As you know, I began writing this book at the start of the UK lockdown in response to the Global Pandemic. Sitting here now on the 22nd July 2020 as lockdown is easing and with the end of Ava's shielding in sight, I can honestly say this lockdown was exactly what I needed.

Looking back to the beginning of March this year, I was again heading towards a burnout; work was busy, the girls were keeping me on my toes and I was starting to feel generally overwhelmed by life again. Therefore, when we went into lockdown, I was given the gift of time. Time to just "be" rather than "do." Time to reconnect with my girls, and time to look within and reconnect with myself. I am extremely grateful that the universe granted me this time, and although I have had ups and downs along the way, coaching calls with Lyndsay have helped keep me grounded and I feel it has done me the world of good and actually accelerated the healing process for me.

The only constant is change and the whole world has been through an unprecedented amount of change over the last few months; we are all now adjusting to what has been dubbed by society as the "new normal." I think what is required from all of us now is to decide what our "new normal" looks like. What do we want to get back to? What do we need to leave behind in our past? What lessons have we learned during this strangest of times? How do we want to show up in the world moving forwards and most importantly what is our real purpose in life and what are we here to be?

Chapter Eight

"I find it amusing that we are all pretending to be normal
when we could be insanely interesting instead."

- Atlas

Normality. It's an interesting concept isn't it? What does it actually mean? That you blend in? That your life follows some kind of pre-determined linear path? That you don't stand out and you just blend in going about your day to day life, as if you are asleep and pre-programmed to achieve certain things at certain times in your life?

Ever since the birth of Ava, I have been forced to sit with this concept of normality and ride out my conditioning around what it means. One of my dearest friends once described Ava as "a beautiful variation" and I have always remembered that as I thought it was such a lovely way to describe her. As I have described previously, Ava was born with a rare genetic condition called Williams Syndrome, which she wasn't diagnosed with until she was fourteen months old.

This came as a huge shock to much of my family, but honestly, the diagnosis of this rare syndrome was a relief for me because I had always known from the days of my pregnancy with her that she was different.

It's a life changing situation to be told your baby has been born with a syndrome so rare that you have never even heard of it and the process you go through as you come to terms with this is a process of grief. You grieve for the child you thought you would have, you grieve for their future, you grieve for their struggles and their differences, but above all, I think you grieve for yourself. Nobody plans to have a child that is born with any kind of syndrome, illness or difference. This is a fact of life. We all hope and pray that our children are going to take on a birth that allows them to have a "normal" life.

In fact, that is often the question I get asked about Ava when I tell people she has Williams Syndrome: "Will she live a normal life?" In the early days, I would go into autopilot mode and answer with such things as "well it's too early to tell really," "she may always need some kind of care…" etc. Now as she grows and is fulfilling her soul's destiny, I say to people, "this is her life, where does normal come into it?" Ava has never known any different. She has always had Williams Syndrome and will always have Williams Syndrome. Therefore, this is the life her soul chose. Similarly, her younger sister, Amelia, has never known any different - her older sister is Ava, who happens to have Williams Syndrome, but we, as a family unit have never known any different. This is us.

I am eternally grateful that Ava's Williams Syndrome affords her little health concerns, and she is a very healthy little girl. She has a mild heart murmur which is completely under control, and she has hyperthyroidism which has been healthily managed since her birth. I know of many families across the world who have lost babies and children born with Williams Syndrome, or have children who are in and out of hospital with medical complications relating to the diagnosis. We are blessed that, so far, we haven't had to endure that pain. Therefore, I can talk about Ava's Williams Syndrome from the perspective of a mother who hasn't had to go through the agony of seeing her child suffer as a result of her diagnosis, but rather a parent who has watched her daughter grow for ten years into a little girl who has taught me a great deal about what life is all about.

I am not going to pretend that having a daughter with Williams Syndrome doesn't present its challenges as a parent - because it does. As she grows, her cognitive functioning is highlighted as being different to her peer group. Academically, she isn't in line with her peers and she does find social interaction with her peers challenging. Ava sees the world differently to the rest of us and that can be a beautiful thing. She is often described as "endearing" because of her friendly and outgoing nature. She makes everyone she meets feel like the most important person in the world, and she only sees the goodness and the kindness in people and the world as a whole.

In an ideal world, this would be perfect and it is often said amongst the Williams Syndrome Community, that if everyone had Williams Syndrome, the world would be a better place, with no division, no wars and no hate. However, this isn't an ideal world and everyone doesn't have Williams Syndrome and so, in the real world, Ava can be extremely vulnerable due to her trusting nature and, therefore, she does require constant care to keep her safe.

As a general rule, Williams Syndrome presents itself with a variety of strengths and challenges within an individual. For example, spatial awareness and fine and gross motor skills can be challenging for people with Williams Syndrome, but they also show a great affiliation to music and singing and possess wonderful rhythm.

Ava is constantly dancing and singing, and you can see her soul come alive when she is listening to a variety of different music. She is fascinated by different cultures and people and shows a genuine interest in learning about others. It really is a joy to watch her. Many songs draw a very strong emotional reaction from her, to the point where, sometimes, when she was a little younger, I would have to switch the radio off if certain songs came on because she would cry hysterically.

One of the recognised symbols for Williams Syndrome is a heart, maybe because babies born with Williams Syndrome tend to have heart complications on a varied scale. Yet, it is also maybe because they have such open hearts and their positive energy radiates out of their faces. Ava has a contagious zest for life and finds joy in the everyday. Don't get me wrong, her anxiety and obsessive need for controlling her future can cause us stress, but on the whole, she just wants to connect with the world and the people around her.

Every family dynamic is unique and brings with it its challenges and rewards. Our family dynamic is that the girls reside with me for most of the week, but still keep regular contact with their dad and stay with him occasionally. From a very early stage, I have been conscious of the fact that Amelia is a sibling of a sister with special needs and this will present her with her own set of challenges and emotions that she will need to work through. Amelia is a beautiful soul and cares for and protects her sister deeply, but I am also consciously aware that I do not want her to feel any unnecessary level of responsibility towards her sister. Despite Ava being older than Amelia, I knew that there would come a time when Amelia's development would "outgrow" Ava's. This time is now.

I wrote this letter to Amelia around a year ago:

Amelia,

I don't give you enough credit. You are just seven years old and already you are one of the toughest girls I know. Whether you are tearing around the place dressed as Spider-Man, using your voice as elected class councillor, or smashing it on the football field or the golf course, or enduring painful laser surgeries, without even so much as a murmur — you make my heart swell with pride.

People looking into our family dynamic often don't realise the daily challenges we face.

However, I know I can always count on you.

You are always in Ava's corner.

You are kind, empathetic and intuitive when it comes to your big sister. You instinctively understand her, truly connect with her, and your unconditional love for her shines through.

You get it – without the need for explanation.

Ava is a joy, but her Williams Syndrome means some days are a struggle for her, and for you.

However, you never flinch in your loyalty, patience and fierce protection of your sister. Watching your daily interactions, makes me confident you will never stop fighting for her and with her.

From the early days, when you would fiercely stand up to children pushing Ava around in the play gym, to yesterday when you held Ava's hand while she cried from overwhelming anxiety – I know you will be there every step of the way as we navigate our non-conventional journey through life together.

Amelia, you are my hero. First and foremost, you are a little girl, who loves to play and have fun, but at the same time you are a resilient and determined little lady, and on a daily basis, even at the tender age of seven, I count on you as my rock.

You make me laugh, you make me think and you make me view the world differently. You help me on a daily basis to keep it all together.

I've always thought of you as an extra special little gift, given the struggles I faced, but just like Ava, you were meant to be; I'd do it all over again in a heartbeat.

I love you little lady – we've got this.

As I said, Amelia is first and foremost an (at the time of writing this) eight-year-old little girl. She is a child. She is growing into her own sense of being and I am very mindful of the fact that I really don't want to cast her in any kind of "role" or create an identity for her other than who she is. In fact, I am mindful of this with both of my children; even more since my spiritual awakening and the healing work I have done on myself.

My girls, like everyone, are unique souls who will find their own way in the world. I remember vividly receiving Ava's diagnosis and catastrophizing about what her future may or may not look like. So many thoughts went though my mind, which I know were probably "only natural" at the time, but they caused me so much unnecessary pain and heartache. Nearly all of the things I worried about haven't happened and I can honestly say that the whole process of having a child diagnosed with a rare syndrome has been a huge opportunity for self-inquiry and growth. However, it is only in the last couple of years, since allowing myself to really slow down and reflect, that I am actually starting to apply the lessons I have learnt.

As I mentioned in an earlier chapter, I had a similar experience when Amelia was born due to quite a large birthmark on the left side of her face. The doctors pointed this out to me straight away and, almost instantly, my anxious mind started to race again. In order for them to ascertain whether the birth mark was simply aesthetic or could potentially be linked to problems with her brain, which can sometimes be the case, she needed to go for a brain scan a few days after her birth. Thankfully, her mark is purely aesthetic and does not course her any cognitive issues at all. However, as her parents, we had a decision to make. We needed to decide if we wanted her to have laser treatment on her face, in order to reduce the appearance of her birth mark.

After some deliberation, we decided we would go ahead with the treatment; as a result, she had her first laser treatment at around four months old. Everything went very smoothly with the treatment, however, it's not a pleasant experience for the patient or the parents. I wasn't really prepared for the first time I saw her after her first treatment and I still vividly remember the shock I felt. The treatment burns the area, and her tiny little face looked like it had been in a fire. Although the doctors reassured me that this would go down, when you first look, it looks so painful and swollen that you think "how will that ever go down?!"

Amelia endured a few more treatments until the age of around six, when she decided herself that she didn't wish to continue with them. Although she is aware of her birthmark, so far it has not bothered her in the slightest. It's part of who she is, and she hasn't once said that she hates it or wishes it wasn't there. For this, I am eternally grateful.

Again, I projected so many of my worries and fears onto the meaning of her birthmark and, again, so far not one of those fears have come true. I would be lying if I said I didn't worry about her being bullied due to it being so prominent on her face. Through self-inquiry, I have realised that a lot of this was my beliefs around what it would mean for her. Yes, we all know that the world can be cruel and there are "haters" out there that can make life hell for people. We all know the teenage years can be particularly hard and Amelia hasn't reached that stage in her life yet. But if her attitude has taught me one thing, it's that the frequency you put out into the world is quite often reflected back to you. Amelia has never once let her birthmark define her; she is a popular little girl, who mixes well with both boys and girls, and she is living her life to the fullest – long may this continue.

Similarly, as Amelia has grown older, she has started to express her own feelings and perspective on having a sister with a rare syndrome. This is a piece she wrote on Friday 28th December 2019 about her sister. I have copied it verbatim, but with spelling errors corrected:

Once upon a time there lived a girl called Ava. This girl has talent. She is a very funny person. Shall I tell you how I know all this? Well I am her sister, so that means that this is a non-fiction book (means it is real) so let's get on with the story, shall we? So, this girl gets frustrated, disappointed and angry because she asks her mum a question every day and if she says, "no not today" or just "no" she goes bonkers, crazy and she puts a paddy on. But, when she asks her mum a question and she says "yes we can" she gets so excited and she runs upstairs into my room and rags me and says, "yes we are doing this today." I am like, "get off me. I am trying to do something, but what are we doing?" "We are going somewhere," she will say, but I say, "but what are we doing?" She says, "we are going to a waterpark. YES! YES! YES! YES! It's going to be exciting and fun." I said, "I know."

What I adore about this piece of writing is that it encapsulates both of their personalities beautifully through the eyes of a child. It is so honest and true. Ava's boundless enthusiasm for life and Amelia's more chilled out approach! It also highlights to me how perceptive children are and how much Amelia connects with Ava in a unique way that nobody else ever will. Amelia sees Ava for who she is and accepts her fully. As is a natural part of growing up and living together with your sibling, they each have their moments of frustration and I am acutely aware of Amelia's need for respite from her sister. Yet, when I see these two together, I know they will not only do just fine in this world, but they will thrive.

The other thing I love about this little insight into Amelia's perception of her sister, is how intuitive it is. Amelia is very creative and she loves to paint and draw. What she has done here, is journal her experiences with her sister in order to tap into what it means for her and their relationship. Journaling is a great way to tap into your intuition and I hope it something Amelia will continue to do. As her parent and guide, I will do my best to ensure she never loses sight of her intuition and knows how to tap into it regularly throughout her life.

Intuition is so powerful and it's a tool we all possess within us. Research has now proven that intuition is a real psychological process where the brain uses past experiences and cues from the self and the environment to make decisions. This happens so quickly that it's not registered on a conscious level. It is a resource we all could and should tap into regularly, to tune into ourselves and to trust ourselves, but we don't always do it. Naturally, I am highly intuitive, but the mistake I have made in the past is ignoring it and labelling it externally as 'anxiety.' What have I learnt, through my own healing journey, is that the less we listen to the voice of intuition, the quieter it gets, until we forget it's there and fall victim to the loud chatter of the egoic mind. I have spoken at length to Lyndsay about this and she continues to offer me intuitive guidance and help me unravel and uncover deeper levels of my being, as I continuously strive to move towards my authenticity and my truth.

Below is Lyndsay's perspective on intuition:

I think one of the biggest questions we need to consider when tapping into our intuition is: What is intuition and what is the mind? What has really helped me on my journey, and I did find this difficult at first, is quietening down the loud mind and tuning into my body and my intuition, which is often quieter and subtler. Many of us find this challenging, because we are all so programmed and conditioned to think that what is in our mind is the truth because we always tend to label that nervous energy that we feel. For example, we want to say, "I feel nervous because my boyfriend didn't text" or "I feel nervous because I don't think I am going to get this job."

How I would explain intuition, is when there is actually no nervousness in the body. I think intuition only comes once and

I think that the way that intuition can really be felt is when you quiet your mind down. So, I feel that meditation daily can really help, because I think a lot of the time when you realise that your conditionings have come from an outside source, when you decondition, I believe that's when you can really hear your intuition speak and it is just a knowing in the body; it's very subtle and it doesn't come from the mind - it comes from the body.

There are so many avenues with intuition and we could talk for hours about it. For me, my intuition never scares me. I think if you feel scared you know it's coming from the mind and when you feel peace and clarity and calmness you know it's your intuition. Anything that is given to you from a guidance level, or a higher self, or your guides is never to frighten you.

Chapter Nine

"To conquer oneself is a greater task than conquering others."

- Buddha

Conquering Oneself. For anyone that has really done the work around this, it's harder than it sounds isn't it? Not everyone will do it in this lifetime, and that's OK. In order for me to grow in this lifetime however, I needed to at least try to do this! I don't think I will ever get to the point in my life where I can say "Yep! Job done. I have conquered myself!" I don't think I ever want to either. Part of our human existence is to constantly change, adapt and grow – life is not stagnant and therefore nor should we be.

Whilst writing this book, I dug out my old journals and it helped me to reflect on what I had managed to conquer so far, up to the present moment of writing this part of my book.

I found this entry from November 2019:

I have been avoiding my feelings of loneliness and lack of self-wroth by repeating self-destructive patterns and surrounding myself with toxic people. The session today at Sacred Moon has opened my eyes to this and made me realise when it comes to relationships, particularly relationships with men, I still have boundary issues that I need to work on.

In order to this I MUST:

- *Continue to surround myself with positive people.*

- *Continue spending time alone doing yoga, meditation, journaling and reflecting.*

- *Continue to go to Sacred Moon.*

My most vulnerable truths are:

- *I have a huge lack of boundaries around men and seek validation from them.*

- *I still feel a little lost.*

- *My lack of confidence and self-worth is still getting in my way, both professionally and personally.*

It's now February 2021 and I realise how far I have come on my journey to conquer myself and my fears. During that point in 2019, I still had work to do around boundaries and my relationship with men, particularly if I was ever going to find a fulfilling and healthy intimate relationship with a male in the future.

Therefore, during a later session with Lyndsay, she commented on the fact that she felt I had a heavy energy surrounding me that needed to be realised, but neither of us were 100% sure what it could be. She suggested I have some Subconscious Healing Therapy. I have to admit I was a little apprehensive, but I trust Lyndsay completely and knew that if I surrendered to it, it would only do me good.

It was one of the most powerful healing experiences of my life!

Before I went, I had no expectations about what this would involve, or whether it would help me or not. However, through this therapy, Lyndsay was able to unlock an incredibly traumatic sexual experience from my teenage years, which I had buried deep and never faced. An experience which undoubtedly played a huge part in my lack of boundaries when it came to male influences in my life. I literally cried and cried as it all came tumbling out, but when I came out of it, I felt completely drained, yet so much lighter. It was an incredible feeling.

It became clear that I was carrying a huge amount of shame around with me as a result of this experience, and this had been with me for over 20 years! My conscious mind wasn't even aware that it was there – but it was and it needed addressing in order for me to heal and move forward into more healthy relationships with men in the future.

Shame. It's such a massive topic isn't it? Again, a lot of the shame we carry around in our bodies is a result of external conditioning. For example, shame around sex and pleasure, shame around putting yourself first, shame around your body, shame around past experiences and past decisions, the list goes on. However, a great way to begin to heal from this is to ask ourselves: Where in my body do I feel this shame? Is it actually my shame? The last question for me is a biggie!! It is so important to separate what is yours and what isn't, and it's not an easy thing to do.

Another example from my journey which demonstrates overcoming shame, is speaking out about my postpartum psychosis. For years, I didn't talk about this huge part of my story. Why? Shame. I felt ashamed that it had happened to me, and I blamed myself for it for many years. I felt like it somehow made me less of mother; the fact that I had missed out on some of the early days with Ava, given our separation, made me feel like I had somehow permanently damaged our bond and possibly her development. This was obviously compounded in the early days, pre-Williams Syndrome diagnosis, when she was labelled as "failing to thrive."

As a new mother you feel like a fish out of water at the best of times, but combine that with a Health Visitor telling you this about your daughter, not listening to any of your concerns, all while you are recovering from psychosis – it's bound to culminate in a feeling of shame. In conjunction with this, much of the literature you read about postpartum mental illness and the impact on the early bounding process makes for very grim reading.

However, it is incredibly important that we do not lose hope during this period and remember that maternal bonding is a process and it is a unique process for every mother. Women have been birthing babies for thousands of years, but nobody has ever experienced the process like how you will - you are the expert in your journey and your body. That said, I can therefore only ever speak from my own personal experiences and perceived reality of events, which is why I have deliberately chosen not to cite any studies in this book (of which there are many).

This is about my personal journey of postpartum mental illness, recovery and motherhood, and no academic study in the world can ever come to close to that for me. I have lived it, breathed it, felt it and I continue to do so every single day of my life. The one thing I can say for sure, is that neither episode of postpartum mental illness has even come close to the bond I now have with my girls. My love for them grows with them every single day.

There is always hope. We can conquer ourselves. We are powerful. We are strong. We are women!

Chapter Ten

"The whole point of lessons is that they are tough. You can call it failure if you want. I call it life."

\- Ant Middleton

Love him or loathe him, you have to admire his straight-talking nature. Reframing failure in this way, has definitely helped me move on and learn from my past and not be afraid to step out of my comfort zone, make mistakes and grow.

I haven't always been a fan of Ant Middleton, but I came across his book, "First Man In" on the book swap shelf at the school where I work and decided to give it a go. I couldn't put it down. I found it raw, honest, inspiring and uplifting. So much so, that I read it aloud to my Year 11 classes along with his next book "The Fear Bubble," which I think resonated even more, particularly with the young people living through a global pandemic.

In 2019, I was refiguring out who I was and how I wanted to move forward with my life. I had successfully started to rebuild my life with my girls. We were settled in our house, I had a job that I loved and I was allowing myself the space to work out how I wanted to grow and expand into my future.

One thing I knew for sure at this point, was that I had to start doing things by myself for myself.

One of my proudest moments of 2019 was when I took part in Ant Middleton's Bootcamp on 3rd November 2019. This may not seem like much to some but, for me, it was massive! Given that I am someone who hasn't always been into fitness and that I am definitely not the army or outdoors type, this was a huge challenge for me. However, my energy felt drawn to it and I knew it was something I really wanted to do.

Nobody I knew at the time wanted to do it with me; the old me would have sacked it off, but this me didn't.

I went and conquered that bootcamp alone.

This is what I wrote in my journal after the event:

Yesterday taught me so much about myself. It was hands down one of the proudest moments of my life. It pushed me physically and mentally, and I learnt so much about myself along the way. I learnt I have lost my confidence, as in I don't trust myself enough, I underestimate myself and I apologise far too much! I learnt I have what it takes within to be and do whatever I want to be and do.

So…who is it I want to be and what do I want to do?

I know I want to inspire, I want to learn and I want to grow. I want to be a leader. I want to continue to push myself and keep moving outside of my comfort zone. I want to be a role model for my girls and show them anything is possible. I want to remain as positive as possible, without repressing my negative emotions, and I want to show up for myself…every…single…day…whatever that looks like.

The only constant is change. Embrace it. Learn from it. Grow with it.

As Ant Middleton said: "Work with fear, use it to your advantage."

That day was more than just a bootcamp for me. It was part of my healing process and a chance to prove to myself that anything is possible. I was so far out of my comfort zone on that day, it was unreal. I vividly remember the run back to base after we had completed all the challenges. I literally remember crying with both exhaustion and pride. At one point, I honestly thought that my legs were going to give way underneath me. I also remember one of the marines saying to me: "Don't give up on yourself." That line in that moment really inspired me to dig deep and finish strong and proud - that's exactly what I did.

Being in the presence of Ant Middleton and his team during that day was truly inspirational and reminded me of the saying, "you become the average of the five people you spend the most time with." For me, being surrounded by all those motivated and supportive individuals allowed me to grow and push myself in ways I never thought possible.

A mantra for life!

Learning and growing from your life's lessons is part of how you prevent yourself from stagnation.

When I left my old life behind three years ago, I let go of a lot of people with it. At the time, I did not realise this was for my greater good. As Iyanla Vanzant writes: ""You have to meet people where they are, and sometimes you have to leave them there." The only way I was truly going to be able to evolve and align with my truth, was to leave everything that was no longer serving me behind, including friendships. At the time, I think this compounded my feelings of loneliness, however, once I realised that this shredding was making space for what was to come in the future, I felt more at peace with it.

The friends I left behind were what I like to call convenience friends. We all have them at one point or another in our life, and again there is no shame around this. These people show up in your life to either teach you something about yourself, or to help you through a difficult time. I am grateful for the lessons from these people, but many of them were more aligned with my ex-husband than myself anyway and so I have never felt like I have missed out by parting ways with them. Nothing that is meant for you will ever pass you by, and I have a few true friends who have been with me since childhood, university and my early 20s.

Those are the friends for every season.

Going back to life lessons. Social conditioning around divorce is that it is a failure. Marriage is difficult, right? You made your choice, for better or worse, and you have to stick with it and make it work, especially if you have children. Looking back, this was probably the reason it took me ten years to finally call time on my marriage. However, when we actually explore this concept, we realise that divorce in fact is not a failure and is often the bravest decision you can make. Once you realise that you are sacrificing yourself to make a marriage work, you realise that by staying you would be failing yourself.

The most important relationship we have is the one with ourselves. It is the foundation on which every other relationship is built and, if you are selling yourself short for the sake of something external, including marriage, then that is the biggest failure in my opinion. It is also unsustainable and only breeds contentment and resentment. My personal experience with separation is that it can actually be the best thing for all parties, including the children. We have had some dark times and making the decision to actually leave took an inner strength, determination and resilience I never thought I had. It has also taken me these last three years to process and work through but, hands down, it was the best decision I made for myself and my family. I do not perceive this as a failure, but one of my biggest life lessons. You are never stuck. No matter how you might feel. There is always a way out from any situation that is not serving you. You just have to trust yourself, trust the universe and take that first step of faith.

Chapter Eleven

"Your happiness should never be in the hands of someone else."

This is massive isn't it? We give so much of ourselves to others, including the power to make us happy. However, whenever we attach our happiness to anything external to ourselves, we are setting ourselves up to fail. Happiness is an inside job, we must first find it within and then share it with those around us. People will come and go in our lives, including our romantic partners, and we have to trust that once this happens, we can still be happy.

I remember when I was seventeen and I had a boyfriend that was much older than me. He had convinced himself that we would be together forever and had pinned all his hopes and dreams of happiness onto me. That was a huge burden for someone so young. When I moved away to University (which he didn't want me to do) and we began to drift apart, he was devastated when I finally decided to call it a day three years later. I remember knowing deep down that this was right decision for me, but also feeling overwhelming guilt about how devasted he was and his claims that he would never get over me.

This example just goes to show how much we do reply on others to validate our happiness. It is only when you allow yourself to spend time alone that you realise that you must be the curator of your own life and that includes your happiness. It is neither self-indulgent or selfish to put your happiness first – this is the only way you will be able to thrive and serve others.

Another way we give away our internal power to make ourselves happy is through our children. I must admit, until it all turned interesting, my life before my children did follow the linear path of marriage, mortgage, children. Society still places a huge emphasis on the idea of children making you happy, especially as a woman. I know childless women of a certain age who are questioned about their lack of children, as if it somehow means they are incapable of living a fulfilling life. My sister, who is now 35 and single without children, does feel this stigma from time to time, and it is both unnecessary and untrue.

As a mother myself, I do relish in the joy that being a mother brings to my life. I am enjoying observing how their lives are evolving and witnessing them as they continue to grow into their individuality. However, they are not my single source of happiness, nor should they be. They are a part of my happiness, and I cannot imagine my life without them, but I cannot put it on them to make me happy. That's both unfair and unobtainable. We are autonomous of each other and we need to find happiness individually within ourselves in order to share it as a family - this might look different for each one of us, in fact it does! This will also evolve as my children grow and I need to be prepared for that. Yes, I birthed them, but they do not belong to me, and it is not their job to do things to make me happy.

This is similar when it comes to romantic relationships too. We place so much emphasis on making each other happy; if we focused on making ourselves happy first, I am sure the latter would fall into place much easier. They say that it is in your relationship with others that you grow the most and learn the most about yourself. I can concur that this has been true for me.

Recently, I have thought about how I might form a meaningful intimate relationship with a man in the future. It was essential for my healing that I did not rush into another relationship straight away but, three years on, it is now something I am starting to ponder. I could easily avoid this area of my life all together and think I will just focus on my girls and my career. However, to me, this feels like avoidance. I believe you can do all the healing in the world in isolation, but you will only truly know if it's worked when you embark on an intimate relationship with another.

Just before the March lockdown in 2020, I had made a connection with a man who I met online, after my friend at work persuaded me to join this dating website for a bit of fun. We had a couple of dates and got on really well. Then lockdown hit which meant that we could no longer meet. He was living in Birmingham and I was in Leeds, so it was very difficult for us to continue to meet and get to know each other. Although this connection didn't last very long, it did encourage me to question my triggers in relationships and work out which parts of myself were still unhealed.

That period of lockdown was a perfect time for me to analyse this, as I realised that through this connection I did still need to heal some shadow parts of myself.

We hear the word "trigger" banded around a lot, but what does it actually mean? I really resonated with Wendy O'Brien's (The Completion Coach) definition in her The Big Shift Programme:

"A trigger is an event that sparks a thought that causes the emotion you experience in your body that has a set of reactions."

One of the most significant lessons for me when I first connected with this man, was that I was still not fully connected to myself and, therefore, I was still seeking fulfilment from outside of myself. I was placing massively high expectations on this connection and I was allowing him to consume my thoughts.

He was becoming yet another distraction from myself.

At this point, I could have blamed him for all of this. Yet, I knew he, like every other human being on the planet, had a story and an internal narrative as a result of this story, and I also knew I couldn't keep getting swept up in projecting my triggers on to him. Therefore, I dug deep and took part in Wendy's The Big Shift programme. I found this invaluable. Below are some of my notes from my journals, as I was undertaking the programme:

What do I need to work on?

Romantic relationships. I have unresolved anger that is triggered by this new male energy in my life. I don't feel seen or heard, and feel like my needs are being ignored.

What can I do?

See and hear myself. Tune into my intuition and meet my own needs.

What do I need from a romantic relationship? What are my expectations?

Someone who adds value to my life, supports my growth and allows me space to be me!

What do I need to release from myself in order to show up healthily in relationships?

Anger from past relationships and shame around sex.

When I originally considered the question: What do I need from a romantic relationship? I realised quite quickly I had no idea and it took me a long time to come up with that single sentence!

That was a big realisation for me right there; if I didn't know what I needed from a relationship, how was I expecting another person to know?

I also flipped it and considered how I wanted to show up in a romantic relationship. I realised, again, that my behaviours were not always aligned with my own beliefs and values. I had written that I wanted space to be me, yet I wasn't allowing this man that space. I wanted someone who adds value to my life, yet I was being horrible, and not really taking an interest in his life at all. I was also plagued by jealousy around his female friends, which came from my unresolved issues surrounding sex and relationships. Ultimately, I had trust issues that were actually nothing to do with this man. He had never once given me a reason not to trust him - I was finding reasons not to trust him and almost sabotaging the relationship intentionally, looking for problems and drama when in fact there weren't any.

Through my own research, I realised that if you have had fairly chaotic relationships in the past, you can find it difficult to settle into one that is in fact healthy and stable. Therefore, you seek out drama and cause chaos intentionally because your subconscious mind is addicted to it. It's a way of connecting with the other person, despite it being unhealthy.

When I reflect on some of behaviours in the early stages of this connection, I realise this is exactly what I was doing. For example, if I didn't receive a message in the morning, I would freak out and send him horrible messages. I am not proud of this behaviour, but it is what I did. The thing is, I didn't want to do it, I didn't like that I was doing it, or the way I felt when I had sent it.

Again, I was allowing an external factor to affect how I felt, and I was putting unrealistic expectations on someone who has their own free will. I was trying to control things outside of my control, which never ends well!

I needed to sit with why I was expecting this man to message me every morning. Was it so that I knew he was thinking about me? Was it a way to control him? These were difficult things I had to work through. But I did, and my own state of mind is much healthier as a result.

The biggest lesson I have learnt, is that no matter what happens in the future, my relationship with myself is the most important one I will ever have. For as long as I am fully grounded and connected to myself, nothing external to me can shake my foundations and I can continue to grow, evolve and transform through each experience I have.

If this man's role in my journey was to simply accelerate my healing around my romantic relationships, then so be it – I am grateful to him for that.

Chapter Twelve

"I am not broken. You are not broken. We are not broken."

For long periods of my life, particularly after my experience of postpartum psychosis, I have grappled with concept that I am broken. Recently, I wrote this poem:

Broken

You may feel you have lost your way slightly.
Your light may not be shining quite so brightly.
You may be feeling out of alignment.
You may need space to be still and silent...

...Please...
...Always remember...

You are not broken.

You may feel you need to take some time to heal.
You may feel you must retreat from the world for a while.

This does not mean that you are broken.

When life becomes overwhelming,
When challenges inevitably show.
Dig deep and use them,
As opportunities grow.

Your wings may be tired.
You may need to take a rest,
In order to fly high again,

And be at your best.

This does not mean that you are broken.

Rather than listen to the external,
Believing we need to be fixed,
Dig deep and journal.

My love, there is no need to cower.
Stand proud in your personal power.

You are not broken.

This concept is not an easy one to grapple with internally, never mind explain, although I am sure it will resonate with many of us. When you go through any kind of traumatic event in your life, it takes time to heal from it and, when your mental health is making you vulnerable, it is almost impossible to make choices for yourself. When I was in the depths of psychosis, I was incredibly vulnerable and could have easily taken my own life. Therefore, I am forever grateful to my family and the nurses and doctors who cared for me and my babies when I couldn't do it for myself.

I know I was one of the lucky ones to make a full recovery (twice) and go on to live my life psychosis free.

However, there is still that niggling feeling I have around choice and control when it comes to mental illness. Although I am not a mental health professional, I understand it must be one of the hardest fields to gather evidence-based medicine, given the nature of mental illness. For example, postpartum psychosis does not show up on brain scans. This is probably one of the reasons that the first psychiatrist who came to visit me on the maternity ward shortly after I had given birth and psychosis was taking hold, was unable to diagnose it in me.

I read an article recently on the BBC website stating that Norway is now offering drug-free treatments to people with psychosis. As the article said, "many people with psychosis find anti-psychotic drugs enable them to live a normal life, however, 20% of patients do not respond well and the results can be life-changing" and not in a positive way.

Reflecting on my own experience with anti-psychotics, this does resonate quite strongly with me. One anti-psychotic made me feel even worse than I was already feeling. Part of the illness, for some people, is a fear of the medication - this was the case for me in the early stages as I feared I was being poisoned. However, even in the depths of despair, I still knew my body better than anyone else and I knew that particular drug was not helping me. I did not want to take it.

After some persuasion, this drug was eventually changed to a different anti-psychotic and doctors reported my complaints as an "idiosyncratic" reaction. But, that's the thing isn't it? We all have idiosyncrasies and, I believe, in the field of mental health, patient choice is incredibly limited due to the nature of the illness. This can lead to even further feelings of despair within yourself, because although you do still know you the best, you are not always listened to or taken seriously.

You are in a Mental Health facility after all; you are broken and you need to be fixed.

As Dr Magnus Hald asserts in the article: "To me the most important thing is that people are allowed to try different kinds of possibilities... it seems that in co-operation with the pharmaceutical industry [patients] have been told things that are not completely correct about how medications work and what the risks are. For instance, there is a myth that there is some kind of chemical imbalance in the brains of people with serious mental problems [and] there is actually no research that really supports this."

When I read this, it was a massive eye opener for me. As I have already stated, the medical explanation of my psychosis has never satisfied me entirely and I have questioned why I was hit by psychosis even further through my spiritual work with Lyndsay. I have come to the realisation that I will never have 100% clarity around why this happened to me, however, it has made me much more open to self-inquiry and not taking what people tell me, including professionals, at face value.

All the professionals at the time told me that my psychosis was brought on by a chemical imbalance in my brain, which was triggered by my birth hormones. This made sense to me because I have only ever been affected by psychosis after the birth of my two children. Therefore, I blindly accepted what they told me and remember feeling grateful that I was able to make a full recovery both times.

However, had I actually made a "full recovery" the first time? Perhaps the reason I became ill the second time was because I had not done any inner healing work between my pregnancies and I became pregnant with Amelia within two years of having Ava. I had simply "put the past behind me" and almost denied it had happened, but I had not dealt with the underlying emotions and feelings surrounding the episode – I had simply buried it, and refused to accept that it would happen a second time.

Given that I was prescribed anti-psychotic medication in the early stages of both of my episodes and the symptoms did subside, I am in no way disputing the place of medicine in the treatment of psychosis, particularly in the initial acute stages. I am intrigued by the research being done by Dr Magnus Hald in Norway into the drug-free treatment. I feel by researching and exploring this option, it can go some way towards improving the lives of psychotic people by giving them more power over their lives. I think this is particularly important in the field of mental health, where patients often feel like all their personal power is lost, and that they have lost control over their lives and their choices.

What I found really poignant from the article was a comment from Malin, who has been suffering with psychosis since the age of twenty one. She said that her "mind was just a blur" whilst on the drugs and since moving to the drug-free treatment she said "I am trying to reconnect with my emotions instead of dulling down the symptoms. We explore what this voice wants and what do I need for him to stop?"

That was such a powerful comment.

I strongly believe mental illness, particularly if it is prolonged and profound, should be treated holistically. Malin's experiences mirror the whole premise of this book, that you cannot ignore your emotions and you cannot numb them forever. At some point, they will resurface and this may be in the form of another psychotic episode.

It seems to me that the work that is being done in Norway is aiming to facilitate patients to find the root cause of their psychosis and why it is showing up for them, in an attempt to curb the reoccurrences. I think this is crucial work, and something that medication alone cannot solve. As I have stated, medication can stop the horrendous symptoms of acute psychosis, such as hallucinations and hearing voices, but it cannot offer an explanation as to what these mean for the individuals experiencing them. I have had an experience of postpartum psychosis, but it will not be the same experience as the lady who was in the next room to me in the Mother and Baby Unit.

Therefore, we need to be strong enough to do the deep healing work ourselves, which can take years and will be, for many of us, a lifelong journey. However, in order to do the deep healing work, we must be able to sit with difficult emotions and ask why they are here and what we can learn from them.

Trust me, when you are being prescribed incredibly powerful anti-psychotic medications, it becomes impossible to think clearly, never mind have clarity around your emotions and feelings. Your emotions are numbed and it actually becomes impossible to feel anything – I don't know about you, but that certainly isn't the way I want to live my life.

As many great thinkers have said, we are not our emotions, we are the silent, non-judgemental observer that sits behind the emotions, questioning what we can learn from them. If we are exposed to very powerful anti-psychotic drugs for a prolonged period of time, they numb our emotions and deprive us of the opportunity to truly connect to our authentic selves.

The role of any mental health professional is not to "fix people" who are not broken, but rather to facilitate their recovery back to themselves by holding a non-judgemental space for them to become more authentically aligned again.

I have done a lot of this work with Lyndsay. Through this and my personal reflections, I have realised that I had repressed my truth for many years and lived out of alignment. I always felt like my life was not my own; I feared judgement, I aimed to please, I often didn't speak up when I wanted to and felt like I didn't have control over the choices I made in my life. This was a part of my childhood and also a big part of marriage and my first pregnancy.

For example, I felt pressured into finding out Ava's biological sex by my ex-husband's family, when I wanted to keep it as a surprise. As I have explained before, I was not strong or confident enough in myself during that part of my life to speak up. Therefore, when I had Ava, it was almost like my mind "checked out" because I couldn't deal with it any longer, almost like when a computer takes a circuit breaker. I needed a ticket out of here, and my mind gave me one!

During the acute stages of psychosis, given you have "checked out" of reality, you have very little awareness of what is actually happening, and it is the people around you who are affected the most. However, once you come out of the other side, that's when it hits you. I have never felt as exhausted, disorientated, sacred and alone as I did when I came out of my psychotic episodes. They really do take a toll on you. Yet it is only then, that you can start doing the work. Although I managed to recover from the psychosis, it's only within the last couple of years that I have fully started to heal inside and find my true self again.

This required more than medication.

It required me to face up to my reality and my past. It required me to take ownership of my life and make changes. It required me to listen to my intuition and trust myself and above all else it required me to be brave.

I am not and never have been broken.

Chapter Thirteen

Human Design – The Swiss Army Knife of Self-Awareness

The Human Design Knowledge is now gaining popularity and there is a wealth of information available around it. Before I embark on my experience of Human Design in this chapter, it is important for me to state that I do not profess to be an expert on this topic - I have not been trained by The International Human Design School. All I can do, is offer my experience of Human Design and how, through my work with Lyndsay and my own research, it has offered me a deeper understanding of what it means to be me.

Most of my research has been based around the "The Definitive Book of Human Design: The Science of Differentiation" as this book was authorised by the founder of Human Design, Ra Uru Hu himself, and contains a wealth of knowledge. In order to fully embody Human Design, it requires one to be fully deconditioned, which takes seven years for an individual to accomplish.

This is not something I can profess to be at this moment!

The reason I chose to include this chapter in my book was to raise awareness of the concept of Human Design as a tool, and invite you, the reader, to explore it further if it resonates and to park it if it does not!

The founder of The Human Design system, Ra Uru Hu, was a successful business man. He was guided to take a step back from his success and the 3D world and went to live in Ibiza. While there, he channelled an eight day long mystical experience in which he downloaded The Human Design Knowledge.

After his intense eight day experience, Ra Uru Hu was able to see that all the information he had channelled was a synthesis of I Ching, Kabalah, Hindu Brahmin, Chakra System and Astrology They had all formed together to create this one system that he would now birth into the world as "The Human Design System."

The concept of Human Design was introduced to me by Lyndsay, and I have her to thank for the title of this chapter. Through our discussions around this topic, it became apparent to both of us, that Human Design is quite often something that is introduced to you by another. It came to me through Lyndsay and to Lyndsay through another. (The other eventually became my partner, as you will read about below!)

When Lyndsay and I have spoken about Human Design, which as a concept can be massively overwhelming, we have both agreed that it is very much a tool in our toolkit of awareness of self and others.

One thing Lyndsay spoke about in terms of Human Design is that during her research, she resonates with the idea that Human Design is an experience, if it works for you then that's great and if it doesn't then get rid of it. Ra Uru Hu wasn't claiming that this is the tool above all tools that will bring us all enlightenment, he made it clear it can be a powerful tool towards connecting with your inner wisdom.

With this in mind, if you do choose to research Human Design further for yourself "you will be embarking on an adventure; a journey of discovery towards fully embodying what it means to be you!" It was an eye-opener for both myself and Lyndsay and allowed us both to go on our own journeys with it, experience living with the awareness of Human Design in our lives and align more fully with ourselves and our truth.

In his own words, Ra Uru Hu describes Human Design as:

"The Human Design System is not a belief system. It does not require that you believe in anything. It is neither stories nor philosophy. It is a concreate map to the nature of being, a mapping of your genetic code. This ability to be able to detail the mechanics of our nature in such depth is obviously profound because it reveals our complete nature in all its subtleties. Human Design opens the door to the potential of self-love, a love of life and the love of others through understanding."

I know that the big question is: Where do I start with Human Design and what can it do for me?

The first thing to do is type your birth data (place, date and time of birth) into The Human Design Bodygraph, which is the software that was received by Ra Uru Hu. This can easily be pulled up online. Overleaf is my Bodygraph:

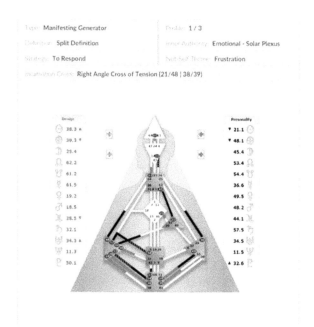

Type: **Manifesting Generator**

Definition: **Split Definition**

Strategy: **To Respond**

Incarnation Cross: **Right Angle Cross of Tension (21/48 | 38/39)**

Profile: **1 / 3**

Inner Authority: **Emotional - Solar Plexus**

Not-Self Theme: **Frustration**

Design		Personality
38.3 ▲		▼ 21.1
39.3 ▼		▼ 48.1
25.4		45.4
62.2		53.4
61.2		54.4
61.5		36.6
19.2		49.5
18.5		48.2
28.5 ▼		44.1
32.1		57.5
36.3 ▲		34.5
11.3		11.5
50.1		▲ 32.6

Confusing right? Of course, you can research and explore the meaning of this energetic map for yourself, and I was grateful that Lyndsay was able to help me to navigate my way through this. I would be lying if I told you that, as I write this, I know what all the information on this map means for me, because I don't! I am still very much in the early days myself. However, what I can say, is that the little knowledge I have of this so far, has already allowed me to shift more into alignment with my true self and what it means to be me!

It is also important to note here that no two bodygraphs will ever be the same, because no two people in the world are the same.

So, what does it mean to "be me" according to my Human Design Chart?

The first area to explore is your type, which appears in the top left of your bodygraph. This is really the lens through which the rest of the bodygraph can be viewed. It is your energetic type and really acts as the doorway to the rest of your bodygraph.

As you can see from my chart, I am a Manifesting Generator – a subtype of a

Generator (there are four types in total.) Through this lens, I am able to note that my aura is open and enveloping and, through my research into what it means to have manifesting generator energy, I was able to reflect on how my life has unfolded so far and what this new lens can offer me in terms of my present and my future. This is the information I took from "The Definitive Book of Human Design:"

As an emotionally defined manifesting generator, I can move quickly into action. I discover through action and learn about life through trial and error. I consciously experiment with life so that others can follow and learn from my discoveries. With maturity, my experiences will cumulate into emotional depth and my personal truth. I pivot through experiences and can move quite quickly from something if my energy is no longer lit up by it. Adventure, determination and exploration are what drive me. I have a desire to do things in my own way. My creative bursts come and go and they are a big part of my life and fuel everything I do. My aura pulls people to me. I don't have "to do" anything. It is built into my design that I will attract the correct relationships, struggles and adventures which will be the grist of my storytelling.

When I read this, I completely resonated with it. One of the big conditionings of my life is that I can be "flaky" moving from one thing to another without always completing things. My path has never been linear, as you can tell from my story, and this has sometimes caused me to worry about the direction of my life. Yet, through the lens of Human Design, I can see that although my journey might not always make sense to others, all of my experiences so far have cumulated in bringing me to this point in my life. Allowing myself to find my own way free from convention not only serves me, but serves everyone around me too.

The next thing to consider in your bodygraph is your Strategy - this is the way the world communicates with your specific type. My type is to respond. This means being open to possibilities and, although on the surface this may seem like I am powerless in my decisions, the opposite is in fact true.

My responses are based on the availability of my sacral energy to connect to and do what I have been asked to do. I often seen this being described as: If it's not a hell yes, it's a no!

However, in addition to waiting to be asked for my energy so that I can respond, I also need to wait for considerable time to know what my actual true response is.

My defined solar plexus is my inner authority and it is emotional. As such, it has a wave that takes time to get to a point of emotional clarity. My truth comes to me over time, when I have had time to ride my emotional wave. Often my initial response is the ultimate one but, by waiting, I gain more information and can allow the correct timing for the action I am about to take to show itself.

Personally, learning about my emotional wave has probably been the biggest learning curve. I can literally go through an entire rainbow of emotions in one hour! Therefore, it can be difficult for me to gain clarity around how I actually feel about a decision, a job, or a relationship. What my reading around Human Design has taught me, is that this is part of my energetic makeup and as a manifesting generator I may never gain 100% clarity, and that's OK! As I write this, I am acutely aware that this may not seem like much to some but, for me, it was a game changer in the way I spoke to myself and how I navigate my emotional wave.

There are also different types of emotional wave; mine is the tribal wave. What this means for me is that it operates through physical touch and sensitivity to needs. This wave builds and builds in me until it explodes and then resets to start the process again. For example, if I don't speak my truth or communicate my needs regularly, especially within intimate relationships, this will not end well. It will end with an emotional outburst from me, which is often completely out of the blue for the recipient.

Therefore, have learnt to share this with the people closest to me, so that we can work together to prevent emotional outbursts. Before I sat with this, I was totally unaware that this was what was happening. In my mind, the emotional outbursts were totally justified and the other person should have seen them coming due to their selfish behaviour! When I have reflected on incidents where this has happened in the past, it has always boiled down to me not communicating my needs effectively and, consequently, acting out of frustration (which incidentally is my not-self theme.) Therefore, I have allowed myself to take ownership of this and accept that it is part of my energetic makeup. It is something that, with awareness and kindness towards myself, I can work on to create more peaceful relationships in my life.

Another thing about the tribal wave that really resonates with me, is that it comes with a feeling of nervousness about revealing who I really am; it can either open or close to intimacy because I never know for certain how to feel about someone or something. This manifests itself in intimate relationships, as I can struggle to allow myself to be vulnerable and fully open to the love of another. As the saying goes, we learn more about ourselves through our relationships with others and, in my experience, this is so true.

After the breakdown of my marriage and my three-year healing process, which will always be ongoing, I came to realise that I was shying away from intimate relationships and was emotionally unavailable.

Without a doubt, I needed to retreat and find my connection to self again, but I am also acutely aware that I cannot and, more importantly, do not want to close off my heart to the love of another in the form of an intimate relationship. Through meeting a man, and him pushing me to dig deep, I slowly started to realise that I can experience the joy of an intimate relationship with another whilst continuing to grow as an individual, even if he wasn't the right fit for me in the end on a romantic level.

This has been and still is the biggest trigger area for me - how I show up in intimate relationships.

Knowing the Human Design of others can be hugely transformational to all kinds of relationships. There are people who use Human Design for Business, Human Design for relationships and Human Design to parent their children.

I believe even a basic awareness of the knowledge can be revolutionary to how you show up in relationships with others.

I would always advocate starting with yourself and what it means for you, before embarking on how this can work for your relationships. For example, you may have a partner who does not connect with Human Design but you do, and as I said before, Human Design should not be something you enforce onto another. Yet, this scenario does not prevent you from exploring your bodygraph and having an awareness of your partner's.

Even without their full engagement, your awareness of both can have a profound effect on the harmony within the relationships.

Similarly, through exploring my daughters' Human Designs (Ava is a projector and Amelia is a generator) this has allowed me to consciously parent them. It has afforded me a deeper understanding of their needs, how they show up based on their design and how our unique energy types intertwine with each other's and impact on each other.

For example, Ava is very open to the energy of the others and will absorb my emotions fully. Now, that's a lot for her to absorb given my emotional wave! By allowing myself to be fully aware of how my emotional wave works, I can ensure, as much as a can within the parameters of being human, that it does not impact negatively on her.

Amelia is a fireball of energy and needs to fall into bed exhausted on an evening, having used up all her energy in ways that light her up. Again, having an awareness of this and sharing it with her, allows us to plan her days together and discuss what truly lights her up, so that she can go to bed satisfied and recharge her generator energy ready for another day.

Ava, on the other hand, is a non-energy being and, therefore, has less energy than myself and her sister; she needs more time to rest and recharge. Projectors are designed to be more open to outside conditioning than other types and I must remember this. I also need to remember that she is not designed to "keep up" energetically with me, or her sister and that her unique gifts as a projector should be nurtured within her to allow her to feel safe to truly be who she is designed to be.

Human Design allows us the opportunity to go deep within ourselves and, as a tool for self-awareness, Human Design really is the Swiss Army Knife!

Let's face it, without awareness what do we really have?

Both myself and Lyndsay, through our own unique journeys with Human Design, agree that it has been empowering and allowed us to reframe our conditioned minds and think of our lives as a series of experiences, recognising there is no need to label these as a good or bad. It is a powerful tool that helps the process of deconditioning. It also allows us to be in the present moment and remember that the present moment is all we have, so why is there a desperate need for certainty?

It is a constant process of evolution and allows us to consider where we have been conditioned throughout our lives and asks us to question where am I out of alignment? Am I on the right path? Where do I need to slow down and reflect?

What Human Design won't do, is give you the answers. Instead, it can act as a facilitator for you to question where you are not living by your design and take control of it.

If Human Design is something that you wish to explore further, just remember you can't do it all at once as it will become overwhelming. Don't fall into the trap of learning all you can without allowing yourself to experience each part. Trust that each part of the Design will unfold itself at the right time and, once you start to align with it, you can't help becoming more curious about its possibilities.

Human Design reminds us not to be sucked into external realities. It invites us to ask ourselves who we are and what we are here for. It also helps us discover what our unique medicine is and how we can share this with the world.

Human Design can give us our unique potential back. It offers hope and it opens us up to others who are living in alignment with their true selves.

The most profound thing that Human Design has done for me, is help me to find and connect to my love. I met Paul in the most beautiful of ways and I am still in awe of how we came together.

Paul is a friend of Lyndsay's and she would often chat about him when we were together, especially in relation to Human Design. He has been on his own self-awareness journey with the knowledge of Human Design and he introduced her to the knowledge.

I distinctly remember the first time I heard her say his name, I felt my intuition kick in – I knew that this person was going to play a part in my journey at some point.

Anyway, time passed and I continued on my own healing journey. Then, one day in May 2021, I went to have a psychic reading from this amazing man in my local town of Morley, Leeds. What he told me was profound on so many levels, but he kept asking me who Paul was and told me that this person was very significant and I would be connecting with him at some point and I needed to look out for him.

By this point, I had forgotten Paul's name and I couldn't think of who this person could be. As I was taking a shower a few days later, it suddenly dawned on me, I wonder what Lyndsay's friend was called again? Was he Paul?

I messaged her and, sure enough, she messaged back saying his name is Paul and that he was single at the moment! I explained what was going on and she said she would call him. As Paul is a projector and very much into his seven years of deconditioning, he was living his life very much through strategy and authority. Therefore, he is required to wait for the invitation when entering into important relationships and, for the past three years, that is what he had been doing.

He asked for my Human Design chart (of course) and then passed his number onto Lyndsay to give to me. I sent him a message inviting him to meet me for coffee, and that was it!

Paul left his ex-wife three years ago and they were divorced in 2020, the same time I had left my ex-husband, and has been very much on his own journey for the past 3 years. Different to mine, but with the same intention of healing and growth. He has two daughters exactly the same age as Ava and Amelia and he is completely emotionally available for all of us.

Given the way we met, and the deep connection we have forged, there is no denying for us that there is something in Human Design. I responded to a feeling in my body and to the psychic's invitation to find Paul and he responded to my invitation to meet. We have both entered into this relationship fully as our authentic selves and in the correct way; we truly are blessed to have found one another at the ages of thirty-nine and forty-five and, as I write this, we are very much at the beginning of what we both know will be a magical journey.

Chapter Fourteen

A New Beginning

It's fitting that I should be writing the concluding chapters of my book at the time of the New Moon in Aries. The perfect time for setting intentions, leaving what no longer serves behind and stepping into the new and exciting energy this moon has to offer. Plus, Aries is my sign and so I am very much at home in this energy!

Last night, I did my New Moon Rituals and channelled this poem:

Plant your seed of challenge,
Allow yourself to rise.

Plant your seed of community,
Bring unity to the tribe.

Plant your seed of communication,
Learn to use your voice.

Plant your seed of intuition,
Know when it's time to shine.

Plant your seed of power,
Know you will be fine.
Plant your seed of grace,
Know you're delicate as a flower.

Plant your seed of joy,
Sprinkled with a little sadness.

Plant your seed of love,
Recognise it's universal.

Plant your seed of alignment,
Know why you were sent.

Plant your seed of wisdom,
Wait for the time to share.

Plant your seed of wealth,
Know you're worthy of it all.

Plant your seeds of healing and hope,
Know that by believing, you are more than capable of achieving.

Plant your seeds Goddess,
And watch them grow!

New beginnings are an interesting concept, aren't they? By definition, we cannot experience new beginnings without something else coming to an end. As I enter the final year of my 30s, and look towards the new beginning of the next decade of my life, I have thought about this idea a lot; reflecting on the significant new beginnings I have embarked on in my life and how they have served me or changed me.

When you live your life through the lens of other people's expectations, quite often your soul purpose gets drowned out by external noise and you stop listening to that little voice of intuition inside you. You may even feel like your decisions are not your own and, as a result, you end up on a path that doesn't align. Your life experiences no longer serve you or nourish you and you find yourself stuck.

During my adult life, I have had a few significant new beginnings. For example, going to university, starting my first teaching job, getting married, having children, and these experiences are all positive ones. However, some of my most powerful new beginnings and opportunities for growth, have actually come from my traumatic experiences. For example, my psychotic episodes served as a significant beginning in my life, the beginning of a life long journey of self-discovery, self-awareness, and the journey to alignment. This, combined with the beginning of my experience as a single mum, have been instrumental in my growth.

There is no doubt in my mind, that the new beginning I embarked upon three years ago, was the catalyst that propelled me into a position where I no longer feel stuck.

It sounds so simple, but when you release the weight of expectation from your shoulders, you feel lighter. When you realise that the path you are on is unique and cannot be compared to others and that you are living within your own time zone, magical transformations can occur.

There were times in my life where I felt like this was it, that I was trapped in this life I had unconsciously created for myself and there was no way out. But, once I had taken the first step and walked away from the relationship which was no longer serving me, slowly and painfully I started to feel less stuck.

What was the biggest thing I did? I took my power back. I stopped ignoring my intuition and I trusted myself and my inner resources.

I have survived: sexual trauma, two acute episodes of post-natal psychosis, emotional and financial abuse, as well as coming to terms with being the parent of a child born into this world with a syndrome I had never even heard of!

For ten years, I remained silent about my experiences with post-natal psychosis through fear, shame and guilt. I tried to bury all the emotions I felt around experiencing this, and vainly attempted to block it out of my mind pretending it never happened. As we all know, that is never a sensible long-term solution!

However, I realise now, that these are the experiences that shaped me and I am much more comfortable talking openly and honestly about them, even if it is still sometimes difficult to do so.

If there is one thing I invite you to do after reading this book, it is to use your voice and talk about your experiences - it is your biggest weapon and it needs to be heard.

Lost and Found

I lost my sense of direction,
Within me it was found.

I lost my sense of self,
Within me it was found.

I lost my personal power,
Within me it was found.

I gave these troves away,
To people please and hide.
I felt lost. I felt hopeless.

I needed to decide.

Am I going to dim my light forever?
In fear it may blind?
Or, am I going to take the plunge,
Surrender and let go of the mind?

I chose to surrender to the Universe.
I purged. I cried. I healed.
I put down my armour and my shield.

I found my voice.
I found my truth.
I found love.
I found abundance,
And
You also have that choice.

Chapter Fifteen

A Different Perspective – Witnessing my sister's psychosis

This chapter has been written by my sister Joanne, who was by my side through the most terrifying times of my life and continues to be so.

12th November 2009 will be a day that is forever etched into my mind. This was the day I became an Auntie for the first time and our beautiful little Ava entered our lives. I remember being so unbelievably excited waiting for her arrival. Emma had already found out she was having a girl and I had been busily planning all the fun things we could do together. I was working as a 999 police call handler at the time, and I remember being at work eagerly checking my phone for any updates. As soon as I received the text to say she was here I immediately asked if I could take some time off, so I could go to the hospital to see her.

I literally couldn't wait to get there!

Upon my arrival at the hospital, I saw my mum and dad. I remember my mum saying to me 'she is an absolutely beautiful baby!' I thought well yeah, you would say that you're her grandma! When I went into the room though and saw Ava in her cot, I knew my mum was right. Ava was the most beautiful baby I had ever seen. She was wrapped up in a yellow blanket and had a little pink knitted hat on.

I later found out that was because she had been born very small, only 5lbs, and was to spend some time in the neonatal unit so she could be monitored. When I held Ava for the first time, I felt a rush of love and emotion I had never felt before. I didn't expect to become so emotional but it was overwhelming. I felt an immediate bond with her that has continued to this day.

When I arrived home my arms were aching - I couldn't understand how they could be, she was as light as a feather so why were my arms aching so much! I must have been holding her so tightly terrified of dropping her.

As Ava had been born so small, Emma had asked me to go shopping to get her some new baby grows because all the ones she had brought were too big. The ones I bought her were 'tiny baby' ones and I remember taking them to the hospital and helping Emma to put Ava in them. She later had her first picture taken in one of the baby grows I had bought for her. My mum has this picture framed in her house and I always remember dressing Ava in it, terrified I would break her little arms or legs!

For the next few days, everything seemed absolutely fine. Although the hospital was a little wary of releasing Ava due to her weight, everything seemed fine with Emma.

This was until I received a call from Emma's husband, asking if my mum and I could come to the hospital - he told me Emma 'wasn't coping'. I was getting ready to go to work at the time and hadn't planned on going to the hospital that day, however, something in his voice made me think I needed to be there.

I told him I could probably come for an hour or so before work and, therefore, set off with my mum to the hospital. When we got there and saw Emma, I was initially quite confused as to what was happening. She was clearly starting to become quite distressed and disorientated. She had convinced herself that she had had twins (I think there were some twins on the ward) and didn't seem to remember that Ava was her baby. She was saying some very odd things and I started to realise that something was clearly not right - this wasn't tiredness or fatigue after the labour, it was something much more serious.

I can't remember exactly what happened next, but Emma ended up sitting outside on a bench with my mum. I was in her room inside the hospital at the time but I could see them both from the window. Emma was very fidgety and was shaking her hands and I could see my mum was panicking and didn't appear to know what to say or do. At this point, Emma stood up and started walking (well, more marching!) away from my mum. It was then I knew I needed to get down to them as quickly as possible. Working for the police, I had a good understanding of mental health issues and the impact they could have. Whilst at the time I didn't know what was wrong with Emma, I knew it was something serious. I ran as fast as I could through the hospital and down the stairs until I got outside and I managed to reach Emma who had been heading for the road. I think she may also have gone into the road at one point as I later found out that someone (I think a passer-by) had contacted the police. To this day I'm not sure how I did this, but I somehow managed to get Emma back into the hospital.

I remember holding her head in my hands, looking directly into her eyes and saying something like 'please come back inside the hospital, please come back in for me'. Her arms and head were shaking almost like she was having a fit, and she was gripping onto my hands so unbelievably tight I thought she was going to break my wrists. Eventually we managed to get her back into the hospital and up to the maternity ward.

The next 24 to 48 hours were nothing short of a living nightmare. I never in a million years expected to be experiencing something so unbelievably terrifying after what had been such a joyous event. Emma's mental health deteriorated rapidly over the next few hours. She was hallucinating, shouting, screaming and just in tremendous distress. She needed to be restrained by staff members for her own safety and her illness seemed to make her even stronger than she already was.

She later told me she had been hearing voices, telling her she needed to die in order to let Ava live - this explained why she was pretending to stab herself with an invisible knife and screaming about death.

At this point we had absolutely no idea what was wrong with Emma and why this was happening to her. She was still on the maternity ward surrounded by expectant mums and new born babies and the staff, as wonderful as they were, also didn't seem to know what was going on (if they did they never explained it to us). I think this is what made the whole experience even more frightening; we didn't understand what was happening, what it was and if she would ever get better.

It was clear that Emma was not in a suitable environment - she needed constant supervision by staff members whilst in her room and these members of staff worked on a maternity ward, they were not trained to deal with the mental health crisis they were faced with. They were however fantastic; I remember them being so kind and supportive and brought a genuine sense of calm over me. I remember one of the ladies (I wish I could remember her name) saying to my mum that she was initially quite frightened of having to stay in a room with Emma as she is quite powerful and strong. However, after she sat and spoke with her when she was calm she realised she was a 'lovely person'. I know one of the things Emma was most worried about when she started to get better, was if she had upset someone with something she had said or done. Even whilst experiencing one of the most acute mental illnesses possible, this comment showed that she had still managed to retain her kindness.

What happened next is extremely blurry and I am unsure of the timeline of events. I remember Emma being visited by a psychiatrist who was asking bizarre questions, such as does she drink alcohol and was she drinking during the pregnancy etc. He also seemed to suggest she was just a bit tired after the labour and left, providing us with no information or idea of what was happening and why. The next thing I remember, we were being told that Emma was going to be transferred to a mental health hospital in Darlington - there were no beds available in the Yorkshire area and this was the nearest one. She was to be transported there via ambulance and I was asked to go in the ambulance with her. Her husband was going to follow behind in his car and my mum and dad were going to take Ava home. It is worth noting here that in and amongst all the chaos and upset of what was happening to Emma, we had a new born baby girl to think about. The hospital were happy to discharge her and there was no reason for her to stay any longer. My mum and dad were given a crash course into looking after babies by the maternity staff before they left as things had dramatically changed since Emma and I were born in the 80s!

I then left the hospital with Emma in the ambulance, but before I did, I was given a huge cuddle by one of the nurses on the ward - she told me everything was going to be ok and not to worry. This was such a comfort to me. I was only 24 time and it was a lot to take in and process.

The journey to Darlington was traumatic and distressing. Emma was laid down on the bed but was trying to get up and out of the back of the ambulance. She was incredibly unwell at this point and it was so sad for me to see her like that. It wasn't supposed to be like this, she was supposed to go home with her husband and beautiful baby girl, not go to a mental health hospital miles away.

Like the nurses on the maternity ward, the paramedics were incredible. When we originally set off, both were sat in the front of the ambulance but as Emma became more and more distressed one of them came into the back with us. He sat with her holding her hand the entire way. He was a calming influence on Emma and me and, again, I wish I had gotten his name so I could have thanked him later. I honestly don't know how we would have got through that journey without him.

As the ambulance was blue lighting at some speed on the motorway and I was sitting side on in the back of the ambulance I started to feel quite nauseous – just to top off what was already a difficult journey, the paramedics had to pull over on the motorway to let me be sick!

When we arrived at the hospital in Darlington we were greeted by the staff and showed to a waiting room. Emma was hallucinating at this point and thought she could see our grandma sat in the corner. Despite the chaos, I immediately got a good feeling about this hospital - the staff were kind and knowledgeable and the atmosphere was peaceful. It was here that I was first told that Emma was suffering from postnatal psychosis; the staff explained that Emma was acutely unwell but she would get better, they just needed to get the balance of her medication right and she would start to come out of the psychosis. I felt such a sense of relief. It was clear that the hospital didn't really want us to hang around but I didn't feel uneasy about that. I was comfortable leaving Emma there, I knew she would be looked after well and would get the help and support she needed. The staff assured me that I could ring at any point to check in on her and again told me not to worry. I left feeling as positive and relaxed as I could have done, I knew she would get better but I had a niggling feeling it might be a long journey.

When Emma's husband and I returned to Yorkshire, I went to their house to collect some clothes for her to take up to the hospital should she need it. I remember going into the bathroom and seeing that Emma had left a jug on the side of the bath ready for bathing Ava when she got home. I felt so sad and emotional at this point, I don't know what it was about seeing the jug at the side of the bath that set me off but it just felt so unfair. Emma had got everything ready in the house for their return from hospital yet it had been so different, in ways we could never have anticipated.

The next few days went by in a blur. My mum and dad were busy looking after Ava and I spent most of my time speaking with the hospital staff trying to understand what had happened and when Emma could come home. The staff there told me Emma was very very unwell and it would take time, but they also told me she would get better. This was comforting to hear, as there were times throughout these few days when I wondered if she would ever be herself again.

It was all such a shock and a lot for all of us to take in.

After a couple of days, the hospital contacted us to advise that there was a bed available at a mental health hospital in Leeds, the Becklin Centre, and Emma would be transported there to continue with her treatment. I don't remember much about Emma's time at this hospital, but I do remember it was here that she started to come out of her psychosis and was scared of her surroundings and where she was. Emma's husband was keen to get her home as quickly as possible and, after a meeting with one of the doctors, it was agreed she would be discharged and would live at our mum and dads house for a while until she felt better. For some reason I was designated the role of Emma's medication expert! I was handed a huge bag full of her medication and was given a crash course in what medication she could take and when; 'This one can be given at night' 'this one can be given in a morning' 'don't give her this one if she's agitated' 'you can cut this one in half if she only needs a small amount'. I felt completely overwhelmed. I was 24 years old and felt like I had been given this huge task of looking after my sister's mental health. I furiously made notes and asked as many questions as I could before leaving. Thank goodness for Google!

From then on, Emma stayed with us at my mum and dads and gradually day by day got better and stronger. I don't remember getting much support at all from medical professionals, it was pretty much down to us and Emma to get her through it. Whilst Emma was at the Becklin Centre, I had heard about a unit called the Mother and Baby Unit which was also in Leeds. It sounded amazing – it was a specialist unit designed to look after new mums who were suffering from post-natal related mental health issues. The best of it was the baby could also go and so there was no detachment from their mum. Unfortunately, as it was so specialised there was only a few beds available and nothing for Emma at this time. I remember thinking it was such a shame she couldn't go there as she would have received bespoke care – she was suffering from an illness that was so incredibly rare she needed trained specialists to help her through it.

As the months went by, Emma gradually started to look and sound like herself again and in February 2011 she told us she was expecting another baby. I had mixed emotions if I'm completely honest, what should have been a really happy moment was tinged with anxiety and worry. This was really soon and the doctor had told Emma not to try for another baby until at least two years; Ava was only 15 months old at this point. I tried to put my worries and concerns to the back of my mind - Emma would be fine, there was no way this would happen again. Everything would be in her notes and the doctors would be sure to look after her, she would be a high-risk case and therefore nothing could go wrong.

On 14th November 2011, our lovely little Amelia arrived into the world. We knew the day she was going to arrive due to Emma needing a caesarean section. I had booked a couple of weeks off work just in case I was needed at home – the niggling doubts hadn't gone away. Emma was released home after a couple of days in the hospital and I remember thinking it seemed quite soon given her history but thought they must have been happy with her. However, in the back of my mind I also knew that the postnatal psychosis was likely to strike approximately four days after the birth – by this point Emma was already at home.

I tried to be at Emma's house as much as I possibly could after Amelia was born. I had been there when she started to become poorly after Ava so I knew I would spot the signs.

On one particular day, we were sitting in her living room with Amelia laying on her soft cushion. Emma's husband was at work and my mum and dad were at the supermarket with Ava. I started to sense that something wasn't right, I could just tell. I knew there was a serious problem when she looked at me and asked if she had been hypnotised. This was something she continually asked when was poorly after having Ava.

My heart sunk.

It was happening again; I was alone with her and Amelia.

It all happened so incredibly fast. Emma went to pick Amelia up and started saying there was something wrong with her, "what's wrong with her?" she kept saying.

I managed to take Amelia away from her and put her in her cot. Emma started shaking at this point and grabbed hold of my hands and squeezed them tightly - this is what she did the first time she was poorly; I knew what was about to happen.

I was trying to secretly text my mum and dad to tell them to come back now, it had happened again, but they were stuck in traffic due to road works. Emma's husband was at work in Bradford, so I knew I had at least half an hour on my own with her until someone else arrived.

I was scared.

What if Emma got a knife and tried to hurt herself, or accidentally hurt me or Amelia? What if I couldn't calm her down?

I never even considered phoning for an ambulance, as I knew that would upset her even more. I just needed to keep her calm and talking, until my mum and dad arrived. I managed to get hold of Emma's husband at work, I told him it had happened again and he needed to get home now. I was angry with him to be honest – why was he even at work so soon after the birth given what happened after Ava? I had taken extra time off work to make sure she was never alone – thank goodness I did.

The next few hours and days were another blur. Mum, dad and Emma's husband all arrived back and I had contacted Emma's doctor to explain what had happened. I can't remember, but I think this Doctor was aligned to the Mother and Baby Unit. A psychiatrist arrived the next day to assess Emma and advised that she needed to be in hospital, there was no way she could stay at home with the babies and get better.

For some reason this seemed to take ages. I'm quite fuzzy on the details but I remember staying at Emma's with my mum and dad for a number of days before she went into hospital. It was a team effort looking after her and the babies. She could never be left alone - not even for a minute. She was constantly wondering around the house scribbling random notes down that made no sense. It's funny now, when I think back, but it wasn't at the time! I wish I had kept some of the notes that she made, they were either premonitions or conspiracy theories!

In some of the lighter moments, me and mum did look at them and tried to have a laugh. It was a little easier this time, we knew what the condition was and we knew she would get better. It was just a matter of time and getting the balance of medication right. What we didn't know however, was how much long-term damage having postnatal psychosis twice in two years would do.

This was a question my dad asked of one of the psychiatrists, his response was honest but frightening – this will have no doubt seriously damaged her long-term mental health.

Emma eventually went into the Mother and Baby Unit that I had heard about the first time she was unwell. I felt relaxed when she was there. Amelia had also gone with her and my mum and dad helped to look after Ava. I visited her several times and was struck by how professional, dedicated and kind the staff were. They were committed to helping their patients get better and were specialists in their role. Emma made friends with some of the other ladies who were there, it was a much calmer environment than the Becklin Centre and the staff understood her and her needs. I later heard that one of the ladies who was there when Emma was, had sadly taken her own life, despite the staff's best efforts, she couldn't make it through. It really hits home how serious this condition, and any mental health condition, is. Emma was one of the lucky ones.

As much as I wanted to be there for Emma and support her as much as I possibly could, the whole experience had taken a lot out of me. I saw things, particularly the first-time around, that shocked me to my core. Seeing my big sister so vulnerable and acutely unwell was quite traumatising to be completely honest. Once I knew she was safe in the Mother and Baby Unit I tried to get on with my own life. I remember visiting Brussels with my then boyfriend around this time but Emma, Ava and Amelia were never far from my thoughts.

That period of time had forged a bond between us that will forever be unbreakable. We went through something in those two years that will never be forgotten.

As a family, we had also faced another challenge prior to Amelia being born. Ava had been diagnosed with Williams Syndrome at one years old. Ava's GP had noticed a few things such as a heart murmur, small birth weight and low thyroxine levels and had begun to piece things together. He believed she had been born was a syndrome of some kind and sent Ava for some tests. The tests confirmed the GP's suspicions and Ava was diagnosed with Williams Syndrome.

Like with post-natal psychosis, none of us had heard of this and we didn't really know how to process this information. Like when Emma was poorly, Google became my best friend! I read so many articles and stories about the syndrome, what does it mean for Ava? How will she live her life etc.?

It was hard for me, as Ava's Auntie, to take in but for Emma, as her mum, who was still recovering from acute mental illness - it must have been unbearable.

As a family, we take each day as a it comes with Ava; we try not to look too far into the future and don't put limitations or restrictions on her. There are so many obstacles she has overcome that at the time we didn't think she would. I remember she really struggled to learn how to walk, due to her balance and core stability not being quite there. I was watching an interview with a British Paralympian, who competed in an equestrian event. He was talking about how he went to horse riding as a child, when he was struggling to learn to walk and it really helped him.

I found an equestrian centre online, which was close to Emma's house, and suggested taking Ava there to see if it helped. The centre specialised in working with adults and children with additional needs, so it seemed a good fit. Within a couple of months, Ava was up and walking, the horse riding had done the trick.

This is just one example of Ava overcoming things she struggled with, she has done this her entire life and supported by her family, she will continue to do so.

Emma is the perfect mum for Ava. She understands her in ways nobody else does, or could. I love Ava to pieces but I'm sometimes guilty of over worrying which can lead to smothering. Emma encourages Ava to be independent and grow into herself. This can be really difficult - it's hard loosening the reins on any child, but with one with complex additional needs, it's even harder. Emma realised a few years ago that over worrying wouldn't do anyone any good. We ultimately want Ava to become as independent as she possibly can, so there are things she needs to learn to do herself. We are so proud of her and all she achieves. She is such a special little girl, who lights up a room and captivates everyone she meets.

Just as Emma is the perfect mum for Ava, Amelia is the perfect little sister. She is such a gentle and caring child and from a very early age, realised Ava often needed help with things; as soon as Amelia was able to help she did. I will often see and hear Amelia doing or saying kind things to Ava. She will help her to get onto a swing without being asked, or help her to fasten her seatbelt. She is also ferociously protective of her older sister and I feel that is something that will stay forever.

Despite being gentle and caring, Amelia can also hold her own! She's a fantastic footballer and plays against girls two or three years older than her. She is a strong and mentally resilient child, who I'm sure will go on to achieve all her dreams in life.

Amelia said something to me a few months ago that has stuck with me 'Auntie Joanne, were you born to be my Auntie?' I sometimes wonder if that is exactly what I was born for.

I have struggled personally with mental health issues over the years and still now experience the odd period of anxiety. I have managed to keep it under control through holistic methods including yoga, meditation and deep breathing exercises. I also know my triggers such as lack of sleep and alcohol, which I try and limit as much as possible. I am very aware of the need to protect my mental health at all costs and it has become a daily habit for me. I avoid situations in which I know I will feel uncomfortable and I don't feel guilty for saying no to something. I am much more grounded now and aware of who I am as a person and what makes me happy.

The experience I went through with Emma, will have no doubt had a lasting impact on me. I'm not sure if I may have experienced some form of PTSD, or whether it contributed to my ongoing battle with anxiety. I never sought any professional help after either incident which, in hindsight, I probably should have done. I have since utilised counselling and medication to help keep me balanced but I now prefer to manage it myself through my tried and tested techniques. It's an ongoing battle but I win most days.

If anyone reading this book is currently supporting a family member through a mental health crisis, I would say to you that it will get better! Your family member will recover and, although it may seem like a long road, they will become themselves again. They will need ongoing support and reassurance that you are there. Don't put any pressure on them to get better quicker or push them to do things they're not comfortable with.

After the psychosis has subsided, there will be a period of anxiety and paranoia. They need a calm and safe space in which to recover and get their strength back, no busy environments or stimulus overload.

Fundamentally, you must look after yourself during this period and maintain your own strength, both physical and mental. You will not be able to support anyone if you're not well yourself, so please be mindful of over giving and doing too much. It's a fine balance and one you need to be very aware of.

Most of all stay positive and keep believing that things will get better.

Chapter Sixteen

A Specialist Perspective on Perinatal Mental Health

I am very honoured and grateful that Deborah Page, who is Specialist Lead Nurse for Perinatal Mental Health Services across Yorkshire and the Humber, has taken the time to write this wonderful chapter about the care that is provided to women, who are suffering with perinatal psychosis. I was lucky to receive the outstanding care outlined below after the birth of Amelia. I can't thank Deborah and her team enough for the support myself and my family received during the most vulnerable time of my life. I asked Deborah some questions and her answers are included in this chapter.

What is your role at the MBU?

I have had the privilege of working in this specialist area of mental health since 2015, where I was lucky enough the be manager at one of the first mother and baby units in the UK, the Channi Kumar Mother and Baby Unit at the Bethlem Royal Hospital, Beckenham Kent. The Unit is named after the consultant perinatal psychiatrist Dr Cahnni Kumar, who along with a number of other contemporary, very passionate and dedicated psychiatrists, recognised the link between childbirth and acute mental illness and the need to ensure that there was specialist provision to treat these women without them being separated from their babies.

When we moved back to my hometown of Leeds in 2010, I took over as the clinical team a manger of what was then, the Leeds Mother and Baby unit and attached Leeds perinatal community team.

As the commissioning of mother and baby units changed in 2013, we expanded, and the small four bedded Leeds mother and baby unit eventually became an eight bedded mother and unit with an attached regional outreach service covering the Yorkshire and Humber region. We have also seen a large investment in our Leeds community perinatal services over recent years. My role is now as the Specialist Leads Nurse covering all three of our services.

Can you describe the work that MBU do and why you believe that it's so vitally important?

Mother and baby units are stand-alone specialist inpatient wards designed to support women in late pregnancy and up to one year postnatally. We know that for some women pregnancy and birth brings the risk of developing a mental health problem. Developing a mental illness at this particularly vulnerable time for both mother and infant can impact on the mother's relationship with her baby as well as her sense of satisfaction and competency as a mother.

A mother and baby unit is designed and staffed with the particular needs of both mother, infant, and the wider family in mind. It is a safe and welcoming space. The Royal College of Psychiatry has designed a set of standards specific to mother and baby units and each unit must meet these standards to be accredited. This gives an additional assurance to women and their families at a time where they may feel extremely vulnerable. Mothers have their own bedrooms equipped with a cot and changing facilities for their baby. Units are equipped with the appropriate range of toys and facilities for new-born babies up to infants reaching their first birthday. As well as facilities for the infant, the mother and baby unit will have a range of communal spaces, and areas designated to therapeutic activities and one to one therapy with trained staff.

A mother and baby unit is staffed by a range of professionals who are there to meet the needs of the mother, the baby, the mother and baby relationship, and the wider family if needed. It will include some or all of the following; a consultant psychiatrist, speciality doctors, psychologists, nurses, health care support workers, social workers, occupational therapists, nursery nurses, peer support workers, with a lived experience of perinatal mental illness, and administrative staff. The staff on a mother and baby unit are trained extensively in a range of therapeutic interventions to support a mother's recovery.

We use a range of treatments and interventions that have been shown by research to help treat mental health disorders in the perinatal period. These include medications, group work, mother infant relationship-based therapies, partner support, couple or family work and individual psychological support or talking therapies as they are commonly known. Each mother's treatment is individual to her particular needs and this in combination with the therapeutic milieu of the ward environment, facilities recovery.

We form a team around the mother and infant. Staff will assist with the care of the infant as required, and through gently building a trusting therapeutic relationship with the mother we collaborate with her on her individualised care and treatment until she is sufficiently recovered to resume all of the care of her baby and begin periods of leave from the inpatient ward, then eventually discharge home.

Our work on the mother and baby unit is delicate, but hugely rewarding.

How many of these specialist units do we have in the UK and how many beds are available? Do you feel this is adequate to meet need?

Since 2011 the work of the Maternal Mental Health Alliance and Action Post-Partum Psychosis, among others, has highlighted inequalities in provision of specialist perinatal services. A 'post code lottery' if you like when it came to mother and baby unit inpatient facilities and specialist perinatal mental health community teams. In 2016, NHS England published its Five Year Forward View for Mental Health. This was supplemented by the 'Implementing The Five Year Forward View for Mental Health,' which outlined the detailed vision for the expansion of perinatal mental health services addressing some of the gaps in specialist service provision, for creating a skilled workforce and targets for the numbers of women receiving specialist treatment and care.

At the time of writing, there are 22 in-patient mother and Baby unit beds across the UK, with Swansea being the latest addition. There are now in the region of 70 specialist perinatal community mental health teams supporting mothers and babies in their own home. There is a proposal for an additional mother and baby within the Yorkshire and Humber region. The majority of mother and baby units have between six and eight beds.

These figures are heartening and a far cry from the early years when the numbers of inpatient units was in single figures. The same also applied to specialist community teams. As mother and baby units are relatively small units, they can be quite expensive to fund. Roughly 1 in 5 new mothers experience a mental health problem in pregnancy, or in the first year after delivery. Between 1 and 2 in 1000 women who have recently given birth will develop a severe, even life-threatening mental illness such as postpartum psychosis, severe depressive illness, or debilitating perinatal anxiety disorder, including perinatal obsessive-compulsive disorder. There is also an increased risk of a significant relapse of a pre-existing mental illness such as schizophrenia and bi-polar disorder.

How common is postnatal psychosis?

One of the first known references to postpartum psychosis was by Hippocrates in the fourth century BC. He hypothesised that the breast milk could be diverted to a woman's brain causing agitation, delirium and mania. In the middle ages, women were thought to be witches if they displayed symptoms that we would consider consistent with postpartum psychosis. We've had a rough ride!

Today, we are for more equipped to spot and treat emerging postpartum psychosis. Roughly 1 in every 1,000 women delivering a baby will develop a postpartum psychosis.

Are there any common factors when it comes to the demographic of women who come into the unit with post-natal psychosis?

There is a recognised correlation between postpartum psychosis and bipolar I type disorder, a schizoaffective disorder, a previous postpartum psychosis yourself, or a history of postpartum psychosis in a close relative.

Some women will develop an acute onset postpartum psychosis within days or the first few weeks of delivery and will not have experienced a mental illness at any other point in their lives.

Mother and baby units admit women from across all cross sections of society. Some of what we term the 'protective factors' against developing a severe mental illness do not seem to have the same protective effect in the perinatal period. Being financially secure, in a stable relationship, being highly educated, and with good familial and social support for example do not seem to prevent the development of postpartum psychosis.

What is the recovery rate for women with psychosis? What are some of the dependency factors involved in this?

Postpartum psychosis is a serious, but treatable illness. The symptoms are often quite apparent and can be very alarming in the first few weeks, but these are the symptoms that often respond well within 2 – 12 weeks to the right combination of medication and specialist support. To recover fully from the psychological impact of a postpartum psychosis and the resulting commonly experienced feelings of anxiety, low mood, and loss of confidence can take a little longer.

The safest and most efficient way to treat an acute postpartum psychosis is on an inpatient mother and baby unit. The illness develops suddenly and can be a rapidly changing clinical picture that is hard to fully assess and treat in a community setting. Once the acute symptoms are subsiding consistently, we can begin short periods of home leave from the inpatient setting, building up to longer periods of leave whilst we 'test' out community support packages, and eventual discharge. Ongoing recovery in the community requires joined up support from specialist professionals and your personal support networks. This will also involve your health visitor, your GP and possibly other social care and voluntary sector groups and organisations.

If a mother has a pre-existing mental illness such as bipolar 1, schizoaffective disorder, or pre-existing serious depressive disorder, recovery can take a little bit longer and require a more intense multi professional support plan post discharge.

What support do women require during and after a psychotic episode?

Each woman experiencing a postpartum psychosis will have different support needs according to her level of insight, or understanding of her illness, social situation, and the severity of her illness. All mothers who have experienced a postpartum psychosis need a safe, non-judgemental space to talk to a trusted professional who can help monitor their progress, provide ongoing encouragement and hope, spot the signs of relapse early, and get the required help if this happens. This may be a community perinatal mental health nurse who will work with the mother at home. Women will most likely be offered ongoing outpatient appointments with a psychiatrist too to monitor their recovery and any prescribed medications, and to reduce them safely under medical supervision over a period of time.

The unconditional care and understanding of family and friends is so precious in helping mothers recover from a postpartum psychosis and rebuild their shattered confidence.

Why is it that the MBU can only offer support to women during the first 12 months after the birth of their baby?

A mother and baby unit is an acute adult mental health ward. Some of the women will be at a stage of their illness, where their symptoms can be a little alarming to a child who is more mobile, aware of their environment and of the behaviour of others around them. It is also very difficult to safely accommodate a mobile infant or toddler who can reach and touch things that may be hazardous to them on an inpatient setting than it is a babe in arms.

When I was suffering the onset of acute post-natal psychosis, three days after the birth of my daughter, I was still in hospital. Yet, nobody in the hospital, including the psychiatrist who came to see me, knew what it was. Why do you think this is and what more can be done to raise awareness? (I know it was ten years ago… so hopefully things have moved on!)

Some of the symptoms of an emerging postpartum psychosis can be mistaken for sleep deprivation and heightened anxiety in a newly delivered mother. It can require detailed questioning and curiosity to spot the early warning signs and all professionals in a maternity setting, mental health, and community health care settings should be aware of the red flags, or early warning signs.

Perinatal Red Flags and Risk Indicators: (Taken from www.dorsethealthcare.nhs.uk)

- Recent significant changes in mental state or emergence of new symptoms.

- New thoughts or acts of violent self-harm.

- New and persistent expressions of incompetency as a mother or estrangement from the infant.

Perinatal risk indicators (Antenatal and postnatal period):

- Women with a history of bipolar disorder, schizophrenia, severe depression, other psychotic disorder or previous inpatient/crisis care should be referred to the perinatal team; this group is at increased risk of severe postpartum episodes.

- Women with a family history of a first degree relative with bipolar disorder or puerperal psychosis should be referred even if presenting with mild symptoms of mental disorder.

- Antenatal presentation can be a predictor for post-natal episode of mental ill health; discuss all antenatal referrals with perinatal team.

- High risk period is 1- 10 days post-natal but the threshold should be lower for women up to 10 weeks postnatally.

- Women who are presenting with uncharacteristic symptoms and marked changes to normal functioning. This can include symptoms of confusion and general perplexity.

- Partner, family or friends report significant change in presentation and acting out of character.

- Older professional women with depression who appear to be functioning at high level.

- Women who present with anxiety/panic attacks or unusual or overvalued ideas (ideas that seem out of context or extreme).

There has been a great deal of training with obstetricians, midwives, health visitors, GP's, and mental health services. This work is ongoing but we are seeing very positive signs and more health and social care professionals are feeling able to ask women about their mental health and their emotional wellbeing during pregnancy and postnatally.

I had never heard of postnatal psychosis during my first pregnancy and it wasn't mentioned at any of my midwife appointments or in any of the baby books I read. Why do you think this is?

Whist it is commonly acknowledged that pregnancy itself and having a baby is a physically demanding time with lots of changes for the pregnant mother before and after the birth, the emotional impact and the risks a woman's mental health were less spoken about socially and at midwifery or obstetric appointments etc. It is often the dominant societal and cultural narrative that having a baby is one of the happiest times of a woman's life. This is something that can influence a mother's expectations of herself and the assumptions of others around the mother, including family, friends, and professionals.

Whilst appointments during a mother's pregnancy historically focused on physical well-being, including the detection of pregnancy related disorders such as gestational diabetes and pre-eclampsia for example, and the healthy growth of baby, there was very little time spent considering the emotional impact and perinatal mental illness. The same was true postnatally. There has been a great deal of investment in the training of all groups of professionals involved in a mother's pregnancy and birth. Midwives now routinely ask a mother about her past and present mental health and emotional wellbeing using specially designed screening questions to pick up any risks or early warning symptoms of mental illness. There are now well-established pathways for professionals to refer women for further assessment, treatment, and support if necessary. These should include clear guidelines for all health care professionals on the protocol for the referral of women urgently for specialist assessment where there are symptoms of an emerging postpartum psychosis.

Public health campaigns have also been helpful in breaking down some of the stigma around perinatal mental health and many antenatal classes now include specific sections on mental health in pregnancy and postnatally. Many also include sessions on understanding your baby's emotional needs as well as their physical development. These can increase a new mother's confidence and sense of competency as well as assisting the delicate process of mother infant bonding.

What message/advice would you have for any women or their families who have experience of perinatal mental illness and who may be going through a tough time and maybe don't know where to turn for help?

Don't be afraid to talk about your emotional and mental health with professionals. Every woman's experience of pregnancy and birth will be unique to them. Pregnancy and birth is a wonderful thing, but it can also be a time for some women that puts them risk of developing a mental illness. Ask for the details of your local perinatal mental health team if you think that you may be at an increased risk of developing a mental illness in pregnancy or after birth. It may be that you will be offered an appointment with a specialist perianal mental health team early in pregnancy, or even when planning your pregnancy if you are at very high risk. There is help out there and it is important to know that you are not on your own. Your GP, midwife, and health visitor can all help you to access enhanced support.

Perinatal mental health services are now routinely asking about a father's / partner's mental health and wellbeing too. It is important to acknowledge that perinatal mental illness can impact on the whole family and not just the mother. Good perinatal mental health services will offer a family additional space to talk about their own experiences, and with the mother's consent, to include them in her care and treatment.

The take home message is that, in time and with the right treatment, a woman can expect to make a full recovery from a postpartum psychosis and other perianal mental illnesses.

Chapter Seventeen

Transformational Toolkit

Everyone finds their own way when it comes to self-care and what resonates with me, may not with you. Guess what?

That's OK!

Over the next few pages, you will find some of my tried and tested self-care tools and a little review of why I like them and why they work for me. There is nothing new in these pages, only my perspective on how they have worked for me during my transformation.

Similarly, this list is by no way exhaustive; I invite you to explore your own self-care rituals with an open mind and heart and if you feel called to try some of these tools for yourself then enjoy your journey of exploration!

Transformational Tool 1: Meditation

People have been doing this for centuries haven't they? No self-care list is complete without a reference to meditation. I have resisted meditation for years, despite numerous invitations from mediums and psychics I have met over the years to embrace it, in order to tap into my psychic abilities and higher self.

My struggle with it was when I tried to sit down in meditation, I always felt like I should be doing something else, and then of course my mind would wander and I would become agitated that I wasn't doing all the things I was thinking about doing during my meditation and would therefore just get up and do the things!

I also struggled to fully be present with my body and my breath, again I would be in my mind questioning myself, "am I doing this right?" "Am I breathing too fast, or too slow?" Then of course my mind would spiral out of control.

My mind was constantly asking questions about meditation and wondering what the actual benefits of it really are.

I think when I finally started to realise that meditation looks and feels different for everyone, my resistance towards it started to fade. Furthermore, once I had worked through my fears of being alone and sitting in quiet reflection, meditation didn't feel as scary. Basically, I let go of any expectations I had around meditation and found my own way with it.

The biggest catalyst for this with me was lockdown and the acute affect this had on the girls and their mental health. We began using guided meditations in the evening together and just snuggling up on the sofa and being still and connected through the shared experience.

This, for me, is where the power of meditation lies.

When you see young children embodying it without expectation and seeing the positive results on their wellbeing, it shows the power of connection to self and others and it highlights that we all have self-soothing abilities within us if we allow ourselves the space to use them.

There is a wealth of ways to introduce meditation into your life, whether that's sitting and listening to a guided meditation, or some mediation music, whether that's meditation in complete silence, meditation in the bath, or the shower, whether it's a walking meditation, a meditation combined with yoga, individual or a group meditation – no one way is better than the other.

Meditation is about bringing you back to the present moment and this can be done in a number of different ways.

As we know meditation is a practice, and if we can see the journey as the reward, rather than an external endpoint or outcome, meditation can be really powerful.

Transformational Tool 2: Yoga

If you had spoken to me three years ago, I would have told you I can't do yoga because it's too slow for me. I need a spin class, or a HIIT class in order to feel connected to my body! When I think about this now, I smile, because yoga has played such a big part in my transformation.

When I was busting my gut in a spin class, although I enjoyed it, it wasn't a way for me to connect to my body. Far from it. In fact, all I was doing was avoiding my connection to myself and body. Anyone who has ever participated in a high intensity class knows they are challenging and therefore you are totally focused on the exercise itself and getting through the class! I still love a high intensity workout, don't get me wrong, but over the past three years, I have found an ultimate amount of joy in the practice of yoga.

My sister has been a fan of yoga for years and would always say how holistically beneficial it was. Therefore, around the time I realised I needed to slow my life down and regroup, I decided to give home yoga classes a go.

I can't say I enjoyed it to begin with because I found it a real challenge. Due to doing lots of intense exercising with very little stretching, my body had pretty much seized up and I was finding it so hard to get into the poses. I became increasingly frustrated and very nearly gave up.

However, when lockdown hit, yoga became my saving grace and I made a promise to myself that at least 15 minutes of yoga each day would be my non-negotiable promise to myself.

For me, yoga allows me the space to connect to my body and feel its power and strength. I love the Yoga with Adriene videos on YouTube, as she is so empowering during the classes speaking positive affirmations and reminding you why you are on the mat in the first place.

It is also a great way to show yourself you can get better at things with patience, commitment and compassion. My improvements have been slow and steady, but I am a million times more confident than I was three years ago when I started on my yoga journey. I also know my body, mind and soul are benefiting from this regular practice.

I am so grateful I found the joy of yoga just in time for it to be an amazing self-care tool during lockdown, and I know it will continue to serve me as we move back towards a faster pace of life again.

Transformational Tool 3: Writing

Writing is such a gift for me; I am grateful for any time I get with a pen and my journal. Writing this book has also been a hugely cathartic experience and I have enjoyed every minute of writing it.

I always feel so much better when I get my thoughts down on paper and it doesn't matter if those thoughts are messy and the writing looks like scrawl because it is a process, a way to release and a way to find clarity. Also, if you keep journals, it is so interesting and enlightening to go back and read them at different stages in your life to see how far you've come, what you've learnt and how you've changed since those entries were made.

There are many ways to write. Some people use guided journals and journal prompts from people that they trust, or some people just write free flow.

I have tried both methods of journaling and, although I often found prompts useful, particularly when I was just starting to journal regularly, now I am much more inclined to pick up a pen, a blank piece of paper, call in my guides and write whatever comes to me.

It is in these moments that I have had the most powerful realisations and it is in these moments that I remember I am part of something so much bigger.

For me, writing allows me to gain clarity around my thoughts and also provides an element of detachment from the thoughts themselves. For example, if I just write without thinking too much about what I am writing and then I look back over what I have written (when I am channelling I can't remember what I have written) I can look at them with more objectively and coach myself through things.

This is where awareness, combined with trusting you have all the answers within helps you to release that, although it's important to have connection with others, it is the connection you have with yourself which is the most crucial.

It is in these moments that you will probably uncover your inner truth, even if it's been buried for years, or you weren't even aware of it until that moment.

Deconditioning to uncover your truths takes a long time, and writing is a great tool to help you on your way.

Transformational Tool 4: Intimacy with self

Yes! This is so important. Whether that be self-massage, masturbation, or self-care rituals, it is so important to be able to find pleasure from your body. In order for us to fully experience sexual connection with another, we have to have taken the time to fully integrate our own sexual energy and be able to appreciate, love and derive pleasure from our bodies.

Even in 2021, there is still a lot of stigma surrounding sex and in particular the female orgasm and women gaining genuine pleasure and satisfaction from sex.

Jake Woodard talks a lot about repressed sexual energy coming from a place of wounded energy; if you are interested in learning more about this and how to balance and work with both your masculine and feminine energies, I strongly suggest you check him out.

Sex should be so much more than mindlessly using another body to masturbate on. But yet, so many of us still haven't integrated our sexual energy enough to fully embody and gain genuine pleasure and satisfaction from intimacy with another.

The first step towards healing this part of ourselves, is to get intimate with ourselves. Get to know our own bodies, explore them, fall in love with them and enjoy them alone, before we offer them to another.

Sex isn't just a physical act, but a deep energetic exchange between two people. When we give ourselves sexually to another, we are imparting our energetic blueprint on them and they on us. This can be either an exhilarating or debilitating exchange depending on where you are at in relation to your sexual energy and your connection with your sexual power. Getting intimate with yourself regularly is an incredibly empowering experience and one that should be celebrated and enjoyed.

Many of us will have so much societal conditioning around sex and, therefore, will have to dig deep with this one, and that's OK. I promise it will be worth it!

If you spend time being intimate with yourself and begin to fully integrate your sexual energy - it will revolutionise your relationship to your body and in turn your sex life with another!

Transformational Tool 5: Emotional Freedom Technique (EFT)

Emotional Freedom Technique (EFT) is an evidence-based self-help therapeutic method and studies into the practice have shown it can have a significant impact on overall mental health and wellbeing. However, you know me by now; I am not a scientist - I learn through trial and error trying things for myself and reflecting on how I feel and if I feel they have impact.

I began using EFT, during the time I was opening up by intuition and connecting more with spirit (something I had been avoiding for most of my life!) I found the practice to be incredibly grounding and indeed freeing. EFT is like anything though it takes regular and committed practice if you are going to feel any benefits.

The first time I was introduced to this technique, I didn't connect to it. However, once I revisited it when I felt ready and set my own mantras around it, I felt I connected with it much better. I repeat the following mantra when I am tapping each point: "Even though I have this fear (insert fear) I trust and honour myself."

THE most important message about all these techniques, is in order to fully connect to them, you must make them your own. People will often question whether they are doing these things "right" and will seek external "experts" to guide them. I would invite you not to do this. I would invite you to listen to your own body - you are your own expert. Nobody knows what it's like to be you. Nobody knows what it feels like to be you, and nobody knows the voice of your soul as well as you do.

Use the power within, and don't ignore that inner voice!

Transformational Tool 6: Sleep Hygiene

Sleep. The most underrated self-care tool there is, and the one, in my opinion, as a society, we take for granted the most.

It is clear how important sleep is to us as human beings, as we know, sleep deprivation is used as a form of torture for prisoners of war!

Therefore, why do we take it for granted?

I think our relationship with sleep stems from our belief system and the external pressures of our current "twenty- four hour society."

Through my experience working with teenagers, it is clear that many of our young people do not have good sleep hygiene; they take their phones to bed with them, they don't go to sleep until the early hours of the morning and they appear to have this constant fear of missing out on something if they sleep through the night.

This ultimately has an impact on their concentration and productivity throughout the day. There have been countless studies that show poor sleep hygiene has a negative impact on brain function, yet our young people still seem to struggle to find themselves a healthy sleep routine.

If we have not had healthy sleep routines in our adolescent years, it is highly likely we will struggle with poor sleep hygiene into adulthood and again this can have a detrimental impact our daily lives.

Even as adults, if we haven't done the work around our inner child healing, we can feel the pressure of the external world and feel like we have to be constantly "on the go" and don't carve out time for sleep.

During my psychosis, as is common, I wasn't sleeping for days on end, and therefore a big part of my recovery was sleeping. Sounds easy right? But it really wasn't. When I had come out of my psychosis, I was left feeling utterly drained, but without the ability to switch my anxious brain off and with one and then two babies to look after. Plus, after having Amelia, the depression set in, and mornings are the absolute worst time, so you don't want to go to sleep because you know you will feel awful the next morning.

It's a vicious circle and, if I am being totally honest, the only thing that got me through that period was time and patience. That's it. It wasn't easy, but it was necessary and the whole experience did make me realise how vital sleep is to our brain function.

Ten years later, when I left my husband, and eventually moved into my own house, I really struggled to be alone on the weekends when the girls weren't with me. Even though my body was crying out for sleep and time in my own energy, I would make plans to go out, just so I didn't have to sit on my own, in my own anxiety.

I could feel I was on a downward spiral at that point, but I wasn't really doing anything about it until I was forced to when lockdown hit, due to the pandemic. It was the best thing that could have happened to me! I was able to regroup, take stock and get some sleep! Lockdown for me, despite the challenges along the way - really accelerated my healing process and allowed me to trust myself again.

For me, sleep hygiene really is a cumulation of the way you live your life and the choices you make. Before lockdown, my sleep was affected by my rising anxiety levels (due to overwhelm and lack of boundaries – see tool number 8!) excessive alcohol consumption, from not wanting to be alone with my thoughts and my fears; classic avoidance strategy! Poor food choices and a reduction in my time in nature and my exercise.

However, lockdown gave me an opportunity for this great reset in my life and I grabbed it with both hands. I reclaimed my power, and started making better choices for myself and my girls. For example, we started exercising regularly again, we took our daily walk in nature, we meditated, we ate a largely healthy diet, I reduced my alcohol intake, I came off Facebook, and guess what? Over time, my quality of sleep greatly improved. It was a process, not a quick fix.

I also made a commitment to myself, that when lockdown ended and everyone was desperate to "get back to normal" I would not be sucked backed into this crazy rushing about, and over committing myself, and so far so good!

In summary, what I have learnt is this: The quality of your sleep is dependent on how much you value and prioritise it and how willing you are to implement the positive changes in your life in order to ensure you sleep well at night and have more enjoyable and productive days!

What small changes can you make to ensure you are giving your body and mind the optimal environment for restful sleep?

Transformational Tool 7: Boundaries

No is a complete sentence. Read that again! The concept of boundaries is a big and complex topic, and again our belief system around boundaries causes a lot of us to have unhealthy ones. Often, through no fault of their own, caregivers and parents, haven't taught us what healthy boundaries look and feel like and therefore we have no way of knowing how to implement them. We spend our lives in "people pleasing" mode, saying yes when we mean no and saying no when we mean yes! This impacts all aspects of our lives, and therefore we need to be clear about what we have the energy for and what we don't.

Being clear around your own intentions and what matters to you is, for me anyway, the first step to being able to set healthy boundaries with others. If you don't know your values, your beliefs, what lights you up, what matters to you and what brings you joy, how can you attract these things into your life?

This is why spending time alone is so important. It might feel scary at first, but it is necessary for you to decondition and get clear about your truth; I promise, the other side is so much brighter and fulfilling.

Setting boundaries between yourself and others can be daunting at first, especially if you are not used to doing it and the people around you aren't used to you setting them. It may even cause a little conflict, especially between families, but as long as you are honouring your truth and it's the right thing for you, then the people who truly love you and have pure intentions will be with you on the other side.

Once you start to implement healthy boundaries and realise that they are essential for your own self-care, it can be transformational. The process will also teach you who is actually in your life for the right reasons and who isn't. It will give you the opportunity to cleanse your inner circle and allow you to really find your tribe.

When you learn to honour your own boundaries, without guilt or shame, your vibration will rise and you will attract and keep the right people in your life.

Remember, your energy is precious and you get to choose who has access to it!

Transformational Tool 8: Spending time in the present moment, in your own energy

I have alluded to this in the other tools, but this is such an important self-care strategy. When we attribute our values to our labels are in society, e.g. parent, carer, teacher, nurse etc. we begin to believe that the only way to have worth is to always be doing, rather than being. Therefore, we may feel that we actually don't have time to just be, which is crazy given the fact we are human beings and not human doings!

However, if we were really paying attention, lockdown 2020/2021 showed us that actually the world still turns when we just are. Life carries on, even when we slow our roll and learnt to be content in the present moment within ourselves.

During the pandemic, we were forced to slow down, hibernate and spend time alone, or with our immediate family or the people we lived with. For many of us, it was a shock to the system, not having anywhere to go, or anything "to do." Many of us could not work, or were made to work from home, which meant a huge gear shift for many of us. We may have felt that life was passing us by, and that we were being treated like prisoners.

Unless…

What if we reframe this experience?

What is it was nature's way of reminding us that all we really have is the present moment and that's all that really matters? What if it was timely reminder that you have everything you need within you to frame your own story? What if rather than feeling like prisoners, we were able to recognise that during that time we were actually the freest we have ever been? Free from expectation, free from demands on our time, free from people pleasing. We were free to be in our own energy, move at our own pace and listen to our hearts and our bodies.

My hope is that those of us who experienced the pandemic of 2020/2021 learn from this experience, and use it to move towards a new paradigm.

Transformational Tool 9: Inquiry with self and others

Self-Inquiry is something that many of us think we do, but actually we don't do it fully. This is because in order to fully connect to self, you have to first decondition from all your past experiences and what you have been told about yourself and the world around you.

As I have talked about previously, none of us can escape conditioning - it's part of the human experience. Once we become aware of it, we are on the first rung of the ladder towards self-inquiry and self-awareness.

The biggest thing about self-inquiry for me, is that you must fully embody what you discover about yourself, as you start to look inward. Each layer you uncover will lead to a deeper layer and each time you pull back a layer you are become more vulnerable. However, if you embody what you learn each time you strip back a layer, you are experiencing a deeper healing and are moving a step closer towards inner peace.

It is easy to fall into the trap of buying book after book in a desperate attempt to find "an answer" and to be "fixed." However, hopefully by this stage in the book, you have realised that even at the times when you feel it, especially in those times, you are never broken and you will not find the answer to inner peace in the external world.

I am not saying don't buy books and don't go talk to therapists or see spiritual healers – I have done all of those things. Just don't give your power over to those tools. Use them on your journey, but remember that you are the expert in your life.

So, what does it mean to fully embody self-inquiry? Well, it can mean different things to different people but, for me, it means honouring my boundaries, knowing what I have the energy for and what I don't and not feeling guilty when

I say no to opportunities that don't light me up. Through my own self-inquiry, I realised my "people pleasing" tendencies were not serving me and, therefore, I needed to embody this and make changes in order to ensure that I didn't keep repeating these old patterns.

This is just one example from my own experiences of embodying what I have learnt. You will have your own.

Once you have spent time in inquiry with yourself and are clear about what you want your life to look and feel like, you can embark on inquiry around your relationship with others. We are tribal beings and are meant to survive in tribes, therefore connection with others is unavoidable; for people like me, this can be the place where you learn the most about yourself and the place that tests your ability to fully embody your truth and act with integrity.

We all have perceived roles to play in society. For me, I am a child, a sister, a mother, an ex-wife, a teacher and a coach. However, somewhere amongst all of those labels, there is my soul. My soul does not recognise those labels and therefore a juxtaposition is created. How do I show up as all of those labels as well as listening to my soul?

Well, I get quiet. I listen to my soul voice that guides me in the ways of being. I am not the first mother ever to walk the face of the Earth, but my soul is unique and my children's soul chose my soul for a reason. Therefore, I have to trust that the Universe has placed those souls in my care because I will know how to raise them.

When I listen to the external chatter or the chatter of my conditioned mind, I get confused, frustrated and anxious. I can take advice from others and listen to them, but the difference for me now is that I trust myself much more. I remember my boundaries and this allows me to get clear about what feels right for me.

It isn't impossible but it is very difficult not to have human interaction on this Earth, and it is something we are hard wired to want and need for our overall wellbeing. For me, the lesson is very clear. Make sure the people you have around you are raising your vibration and not lowering it, that they have good intentions for themselves and you and that they have done the work to raise their vibration in order to also live their best life.

When humans connect authentically and for the greater good, this is when they can change the world!

Transformational Tool Number 10:

Make time for fun and play! Give yourself permission to have fun and do what lights your soul up, whether that's singing, dancing, playing with your children, skateboarding, trampolining or anything else that takes your fancy! Tune into your inner child, ask them what they need and listen to the answer!

Final Thoughts
Why Me?

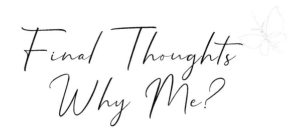

For a year and half, I have been writing this book and I am so proud to be writing my final thoughts and sharing them with you.

For me, writing this book has proven to be a hugely cathartic experience and for the process alone, I am eternally grateful.

After the birth of Ava, and during my recovery from psychosis, I would often think to myself - why me? Why was I the one who suffered such trauma at a time which is supposed to be one of the most magical times of your life? I used to think I was being punished in some way, or that I was a bad person, and perhaps this was the universe's way of punishing me and telling me I am not fit to be parent.

Reflecting on these thoughts now, I realise how self-destructive they were and I have spent much of the last ten years working on reframing this internal narrative to something more positive.

The question why me? Now leads to much more positive responses. I believe my experiences of psychosis were a form of purging; I had been holding on to so much internally and not allowing my authentic self to shine through in order to please others. After the birth of Amelia, the same thing happened again because I had not learnt my lesson the first time!

I now truly believe that these experiences, however painful, are sent for us to grow, learn and connect to our higher self.

What is life really? Life is a set of experiences that we grow through and expand. We either choose to take the lessons from each experience and transcend the ego or we remain stuck in our own self-destructive patterns and belief systems.

The only constant is change and life is never static. We have to experience the highs and the lows to have an authentic, rich and genuine human experience.

Recently, I have been exploring my own connection to Spirit and spending much more time in meditation and quiet reflection. This has helped me even more in my journey towards self-awareness.

I had found myself becoming triggered in some of my coaching sessions and also around my soon to be ex-husband's new partner; therefore, I knew I needed to go into these feelings and open up to the guidance of Spirit.

What they told me and what I wrote down in my journal is this:

"We need you to transcend the ego and operate from a place of higher consciousness. We need you to see only souls. Tap into energy and souls. We don't care what they think, and neither should you! You have nothing to prove – that's ego!"

Therefore, the main point of the message, for me, was that I do sometimes operate from a place of comparison, which comes from my body image wounds and a place of trying to prove I can "fix" people, which in turn comes from the massively high expectations I place on myself and my need to prove my worth.

Even after three years of doing the inner work, I am still learning and transcending different parts of myself and I love it!

I never want to remain static and I never want to stop learning and growing through this human experience.

What are we all really craving? Well, to me, we are craving contentment and inner peace. Happiness feels like inner peace. Happiness has always been an inside job and it ebbs and flows, as life does.

We are all part of something greater and we are all connected. I believe what our souls truly crave is Oneness. Oneness with self, oneness with each other and oneness with every other aspect of the universe. However, you can only begin to come close to experiencing this, if you feel at one with yourself first.

Oneness

Transcend the mind,
Which divides and separates,
And be at One.
Be at One with your body, with your soul and with your higher self.
Be at One with the world around you,
With other people and with Mother Earth.
Be at One with the ebb and flow of life,
With the experiences and emotions that it brings.

Be at One with yourself.

Integrate your past,
And Be at One with the memories.
Be at One with the present,
Be at One with the Universe
And trust what's to come.

Be at One.

About the Author:
Who am I?

Emma Louise Daniels is an author, teacher and coach. She has worked in education for over 15 years and is the founder of Transforming Mindsets, which offers holistic coaching programmes to individuals and groups.

Emma is a single mum of two daughters, one of whom has Williams Syndrome. She is a passionate advocate for inclusion, support for parents of children with complex needs and mental health awareness.

To contact Emma, you can visit her on Instagram or Twitter:

@transforming_mindsets

@Empaps

Further Reading and References

Ant, M., 2018. *First Man In: Leading from the Front*. London: HarperCollins .

Ant, M., 2020. *The Fear Bubble: Harness your Fear and Live Without Limits*. London : HarperCollins .

Bessel, K. V. D., 2015. *The Body Keeps the Score: Mind, brain and body in the transformation of trauma*. Third Edition ed. London : Penguin Books .

Brene, B., 2015. *Daring Greatly: How the Courage to Be Vulnerable Transforms the Way We Live, Love, Parent, and Lead*. London : Penguin Life .

Catherine, G., 2017. *The Unexpected Joy of Being Sober: Discovering a happy, healthy, wealthy alcohol free life*. London : Aster.

Kirsty, G., 2020. *Lunar Living: Working with the Magic of the Moon Cycles*. London : Yellow Kite .

Lynda, B., 2017. *The Definitve Book of Human Design: The Science of Differentiation*. Third ed. Carlsbad: HDC Publishing .

Michael, S., 2015. *The Untethered Soul: The Journey Beyond Yourself*. London : Eureka Books .

Sylvia, P., 2001. *The Bell Jar*. Main- Re-issue ed. London : Faber and Faber .

Find: Jake Woodard on Instagram @_jakewoodard

Find: Wendy O'Brien The Completion Coach on Instagram @thecompletioncoach

Find Lyndsay Adele Agus - Sacred Moon Wellbeing Centre at her website: https://sacredmoon.co/

Never Lose Your Connection to you Inner Child!

Go Out and Play!